THE
10-STEP
STRESS
SOLUTION

THE
10-STEP
STRESS
SOLUTION

Live More,
Relax More,
Reenergize

NEIL SHAH

TARCHER/PENGUIN
a member of Penguin Group (USA)
New York

JEREMY P. TARCHER/PENGUIN
Published by the Penguin Group
Penguin Group (USA) LLC
375 Hudson Street
New York, New York 10014

USA · Canada · UK · Ireland · Australia
New Zealand · India · South Africa · China

penguin.com
A Penguin Random House Company

First published in the United Kingdom by Vermilion in 2012
First Tarcher/Penguin paperback edition published in 2013
Copyright © 2012 by Neil Shah

Most Tarcher/Penguin books are available at special quantity discounts
for bulk purchase for sales promotions, premiums, fund-raising, and
educational needs. Special books or book excerpts also can be created to fit
specific needs. For details, write: Special.Markets@us.penguingroup.com.

Library of Congress Cataloging-in-Publication Data

Shah, Neil.
The 10-step stress solution : live more, relax more, reenergize / Neil Shah.
p.   cm.
Includes index.
ISBN 978-0-399-16607-5
1. Stress (Psychology).   2. Stress management.   3. Time management.
I. Title.   II. Title: Ten steps stress solution.
BF575.S75S482   2013   2013028975
155.9'042—dc23

I dedicate this book to you, Dad;
I couldn't have got here without you!

CONTENTS

Introduction   1

PART 1: EXPLAINING STRESS

Chapter 1   What is stress?   8
Chapter 2   How stress affects the body   13
Chapter 3   The slavery of stress   28
Chapter 4   Coping with stress   35

PART 2: THE 10-STEP STRESS SOLUTION

Chapter 5   Step 1: Prioritize your health   46
Chapter 6   Step 2: Get a good night's sleep   55
Chapter 7   Step 3: Practice deep breathing   71
Chapter 8   Step 4: Stay hydrated   87
Chapter 9   Step 5: Eat for well-being NOT for stress   94
Chapter 10   Step 6: Get moving to combat stress   107
Chapter 11   Step 7: Adopt a positive mindset   118
Chapter 12   Step 8: Be the master of your time   133
Chapter 13   Step 9: Don't be a slave to technology—master it   146
Chapter 14   Step 10: Learn to say no   158
Chapter 15   Putting the 10-step stress solution into action   168

Further support   175
Acknowledgments   176
Index   177
About the author   184

INTRODUCTION

What is stress? These days you can't turn on the television or radio, or pick up a newspaper or magazine without people going on about stress. And if they are not directly talking about stress, it's likely they are giving you some information that is going to get you stressed—the failing global economy, war, terrorism, climate challenges, murder, your sports team's poor results . . .

We live in a stressful era, possibly the most stressful period humans have ever experienced, and stress is one of the biggest issues that modern man has to deal with. Contributing to myriad illnesses, some of which even lead to death, it is a state that costs companies and our economies billions.

It is something that everyone can relate to. When I tell people I work in stress management, the vast majority of people respond with, "I need some of that!"

If I ask a roomful of people how many of them are concerned about the impact that stress has on their health, well-being, relationships and ability to focus at work, most will hold their hands up. Would you?

Even though stress is something we can all relate to, have probably all experienced and are likely to be concerned by, most of us do not really understand what it is. We are ill-equipped to recognize it and therefore to take steps to minimize its negative effects.

Stress can be the driving force that keeps us on our toes and ensures we push ourselves to be the best we can be. However, if we have too much stress, it can drive us into physical, mental and emotional exhaustion. Therefore we need to strike the right balance. Certainly we can't avoid the problem; situations arise on a daily basis that make physical, mental and emotional demands on us: there may be decisions to be made, deadlines to be met, lessons to be learned; but as individuals, we must take stock of all aspects of our life and situations and learn to cope better. Treat stress early, and your prospects are good. But ignore the problem, and there is a risk that "burnout" may become a permanent state of affairs. Unreasonable stress affects one in five of the population, so a sensible response would be to learn to manage it better.

WHAT THIS BOOK OFFERS

This book will begin to teach you what we should all have been taught as children—how to manage stress and ensure that we are able to recognize when we are in a state of stress and be able to take the steps to change our behavior quickly. It is designed to give you some of the answers, to empower and enlighten you. The book contains a simple 10-step process, written in plain English, without jargon or technical language. It also includes background information about stress, plus some practical suggestions on diet, relaxation and lifestyle changes. It has been written to give you simple, practical knowledge and techniques that will enable you to take back control of your life.

I have 10 years of experience, knowledge and expertise in stress management—gained from working with some leading health and well-being professionals coupled with hands-on experience of delivering projects across the world, allowing me to gain a vast range of experience with people from a broad spectrum of industries, cultures and environments. This has allowed me to understand some of the core common challenges that we face today and to develop some powerful solutions to cope with these challenges as well as to increase our resilience to the pressures of modern life. This isn't just another "do this and your life will be amazing" self-help book. Most of the information offered in these pages has been gained from personal, firsthand experience: my first stressed-out, on-the-brink-of-a-breakdown client was myself.

WHAT QUALIFIES ME TO WRITE THIS BOOK?

Today I am happy, healthy, calm and relaxed. I have an abundance of energy, which I have used for various things from running the London marathon four times to climbing mountains. I am also the founder and director of The Stress Management Society, an organization dedicated to helping people tackle stress, and one of the UK's leading authorities on stress-management issues. I successfully run three other companies, all focused on health, well-being, stress reduction and success achievement. I am seen as an expert in stress reduction and relaxation by my peers. I have a wonderful team, amazing friends and an incredible family.

But it was only 10 years ago that my previous company failed. I had started an IT recruitment firm at the age of 24 and turned it into a multimillion-dollar business. I had offices in London and South Africa, a string of awards including Shell LiveWIRE Young Entrepreneur of the Year, the Success through People award, nominations for the DTI/EU "Best European Small Business Initiative" and had achieved the Investors in People standard in record time. My success had even attracted an invitation to 10 Downing Street to meet the then prime minister, Tony Blair.

However, being young and naive, I made some poor decisions along the way, which wasn't too much of a problem when the going was good; however, when the dot.com bubble burst and the business climate changed, I found that my choices were testing both the business and myself. I found myself struggling: I couldn't focus at work, I was spending longer and longer in the office, I couldn't sleep at night and I was always angry. I was overwhelmed and under pressure and simply not coping. I didn't recognize this as stress; however, I knew I needed help. I made an appointment to see my doctor, who after listening to me for a few minutes suggested that antidepressants might help me to cope with some of the symptoms I was experiencing. Now, I knew enough to know that this wasn't the answer. I asked if he had any other suggestions and he recommended I book an appointment to see a therapist.

During the appointment I had 45 minutes to talk about my concerns and challenges and how I felt. It felt good to get things off my chest; however, the therapist's response at the end left me a little dismayed. Essentially, she thought I was "young, fit and healthy" and that there were people with far worse problems than me. I am sure that whatever she said was an attempt to get me to put things into some kind of perspective; however, I wasn't prepared to accept this and wanted to continue to seek a means of helping myself deal with the stress I was experiencing. Yet I couldn't find anything or anyone to give me the specific support I needed.

In the end I made the difficult decision to put my business into bankruptcy. I had to hold my hands up and say "I cannot continue to run this business," which led to administrators taking over and the business ceasing trading. We had debts and plenty of creditors chasing money, plus staff who needed to be informed, and I found myself on the verge of a breakdown. I was extremely stressed, exhausted and depressed and I was ill and completely burned out. I had lost everything—my appetite, my sex drive, my money, my car and even a lot of people whom I considered to be my close friends. I was frustrated, lacking focus and was struggling to keep my life together. I didn't know how to deal with it and I felt helpless. I was in the lowest place I had ever been in my life. I tried therapy, life coaches, counselors and healers. At one point I even turned to the antidepressants that I had previously rejected, but nothing worked!

WHAT CHANGED MY LIFE

I made the decision that I needed to get back on top of my life and on top of the world—so I traveled to the Himalayas with the intention of climbing Mount Everest. I needed a mission to refocus my mind and a goal to distract me from the challenges in my life. I needed a time-out from my problems. It was a life-changing experience—as William Blake said, "Great things are done when men and mountains meet. This is not done by jostling in the street." I learned much about myself and even had an opportunity to spend some time in a monastery with some Buddhist monks, hearing their astonishing ancient secrets. That experience and those secrets enabled me to turn my life around and got me to where I am now. I wanted to use my experiences and turn them into something positive. I knew that there was a lack of resources for adults feeling burdened by stress and I wanted to fill that gap. It was then that I decided to set up The Stress Management Society. Today, I am committed to sharing what I have learned with others and, through the organization, to providing support, guidance and assistance to those in need of help—both individuals and companies.

PART 1
EXPLAINING STRESS

CHAPTER 1

WHAT IS STRESS?

Many of you bought this book because you need solutions to your stress; you want tips and techniques to help you cope. However, first you need to have a better understanding of what stress is and how it manifests itself in your life, because without understanding the question the answer may not make much sense. So let's start with some background knowledge.

DEFINING STRESS

Stress. We all suffer from it and know what it feels like. So you'd think it'd be easy to define. But finding an adequate definition is harder than you think. Scientists have certainly tried. Over the last 100 years much research has been conducted into stress in order to define it accurately and at times we've seen the scientific equivalent of open warfare between those holding competing theories and definitions. Some of these theories have been debunked over time, but a couple still hold fast.

Fight or flight

Walter Cannon's early research on stress in 1932 established the existence of the "fight-or-flight response." It is our body's primitive, automatic response that prepares the body to "fight" or "flee" from perceived attack or harm. Cannon showed that when an organism experiences a shock or perceives a threat, it quickly releases hormones that help it to survive. In humans, as in animals, these hormones help the organism to run faster and fight harder. They increase heart rate and blood pressure, delivering more oxygen and blood sugar to power important muscles. They increase sweating in an effort to cool these muscles and to help them stay efficient. They divert blood away from the skin to the core of our bodies, reducing blood loss if we are damaged. As well as this, these hormones focus our attention on the threat, to the exclusion of everything else.

So what is the point of stress? Why do we have it? For the answer to this, we have to look at how we as a species evolved. Modern humans first surfaced in Africa approximately 200,000 years ago. One of those early humans was one of our common ancestors, a guy called Caveman Joe. Caveman Joe was strolling through the jungle one day on his way back to the cave when all of a sudden a sabertooth tiger pounced out from behind a bush. Faced with the impending threat of the sabertooth tiger, Joe went into a fight-or-flight state. His body prepared itself to defend and attack. For Joe, this was a useful response—his life was being threatened by the tiger and the stress helped him act fast.

Yet it's not just life-threatening events that trigger this reaction. Even relatively minor frustrations or unexpected events can prompt it, although when the threat is small, our response is small. Therefore we often may not notice it amid the many other distractions of a stressful situation.

A positive force

Dr. Hans Selye was another founding father of stress research. His research led him to conclude that the biochemical effects of stress would be experienced, irrespective of whether the situation was positive or negative. He went even further, stating that, "stress is not necessarily something bad—it all depends on how you take it. The stress of exhilarating, creative successful work is beneficial, while that of failure, humiliation or infection is detrimental." Today, stress is viewed as a "bad thing," with a range of harmful biochemical and long-term effects. These effects have rarely been observed in positive situations. However, there are many experiences where stress (or a degree of it) will serve you to perform to the best of your ability.

A modern definition

A popular modern definition of stress is that stress is a condition or feeling experienced when a person perceives that demands exceed the personal and social resources the individual is able to mobilize. In addition, there is an intertwined instinctive stress response to unexpected events. The stress response inside us is therefore part instinct and part to do with the way we respond to situations.

When I formed The Stress Management Society in 2003 I had communicated with many of the authorities and agencies that were involved in dealing with stress. I spoke with the NHS, the Health and Safety Executive and even several universities that were researching stress. I was fascinated to learn that everyone seemed to have their own definition of stress, and it became apparent that the experts didn't all agree on a common definition. This was a real cause of concern for me, as if the experts didn't agree then that would be a real challenge for the lay person who was trying to get their head around what stress actually is. Yet while doing my research I happened to be introduced to a structural engineer who knew a lot about stress, not so much to people, but to bridges, buildings and metal. I was fascinated by his take on stress. In fact his definition was so clear and powerful that we ended up using it within our organization.

The bridge metaphor

I would like you to imagine a bridge. Then imagine driving lots of double-decker buses onto the bridge, until it is completely covered with them. Then, using a crane, imagine placing lots of trucks filled with concrete on top of the buses. Top them with a cargo ship filled with oil. Then place a couple of Boeing 747s on the ship, then a few helicopters, maybe a dozen tanks . . . If you put enough weight on the bridge what will happen?

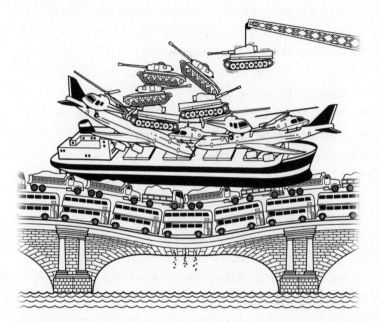

That's right, eventually it will collapse under the load. However, before it collapses how do we know it's not doing too well? It will begin to bow, buckle, groan and creak. And when the bridge is giving us the clues that it's not coping, we have a couple of choices to prevent it from collapsing.

1) We can remove some of the load, and/or
2) We can give the bridge some additional support, maybe by using concrete blocks or iron girders to increase the structural integrity of the bridge so it is better equipped to cope with the load.

Now, when the engineer described stress to me I immediately realized that people are exactly the same. If you put enough demand (or apply enough pressure) on a person, they, too, will collapse like a bridge. What are the effects of a person collapsing? They can be mental, emotional and physical. However, just like the bridge, before the person collapses there will be some bowing, buckling, groaning and creaking—signs of stress. We are all impacted by stress in different ways, but these signs could include:

- Being accident prone
- Feeling argumentative and snappy
- A tendency to work late and not take breaks
- Indecisiveness and poor judgment
- A loss of sense of humor, replaced by irritability
- Losing pride in one's appearance
- A tendency to suffer from headaches, nausea, aches and pains, tiredness and poor sleeping patterns
- Needing time off work
- A problem with drinking, smoking, overeating or drug taking

This bridge metaphor can be very helpful when you are in a stressful situation. You might find it useful to visualize your own bridge, with all of your own various pressures piled up on it. What pressures do you have to deal with? Can your bridge cope under all that weight? You can then work out whether you can strengthen your supports or take off some of the pressure. The 10-step program in this book will show you how you can take measures to do this.

CHAPTER 2

HOW STRESS AFFECTS THE BODY

Causes of stress are known as stressors. They can be internal (for example, infection, inflammation, an anxious outlook or a poor diet) or external (such as stressful working conditions or bullying). Stressors can also be either short term or long term. A short-term "acute" stressor is an immediate threat, and the body reacts to it with the fight-or-flight response (see pages 8–9). When the threat subsides, the body returns to normal. Long-term or "chronic" stressors are pressures that don't quickly subside. These are particularly worrying because they are the ones that cause lasting damage to the body.

In modern life, we have no shortage of short-term stress in our lives. We may get stuck in a traffic jam, argue with a colleague at work or put up with the in-laws for Christmas. But much of our stress is chronic in nature—the result of working long hours at a demanding job, caring for an aging parent or even recovering from surgery.

PROGRESSION OF STRESS

When we experience short- or long-term stress, we progress through three specific stages: "alarm," "resistance" and "exhaustion." If we are able to recognize the early signs of stress, we can prevent it from progressing and having a deeper impact on our lives and well-being.

Stage 1: ALARM

This could be triggered by an unexpected stressor, such as a saber-tooth tiger attack (think of Caveman Joe from Chapter 1), an accident or some external threat or challenge. Alternatively it could be triggered by a cause of stress that was foreseen—stressors such as a job interview, speaking in public, an examination or getting married.

When you face a danger or threat, your nervous system immediately sends an SOS signal to your brain. You go into a state of readiness, you are hyperstimulated and your body is physically prepared to take whatever action is necessary to address the threat or danger. Often the first reaction is a feeling of tension, apprehension and worry, which are clearly visible in your face. Then we see behavioral and physiological changes, such as trembling, palpitations or dizziness plus symptoms of anxiety. This is your bridge beginning to bow and buckle, and as this happens you might experience:

- An increased heart rate
- A dry mouth
- A tense forehead
- Shallow and fast breathing
- Clenched jaws and teeth
- Flushing of the face
- Feelings of anger or hostility
- Increased perspiration
- Tightness of the skin
- Increased blood sugar
- Increased blood pressure
- Suspension of the digestive system and "butterflies" in the stomach
- A relaxed bladder

Stay in this state for a prolonged period and all your energy goes to dealing with regulating these body changes. Physically you end up exhausted.

Stage 2: RESISTANCE

When the cause of stress is not addressed and you stay in stage 1 for extended periods, your energy levels begin to diminish. Our bodies were only ever designed to use stress as a short-term intervention, so your body has to work extremely hard to maintain itself in a state of stress. If we do not take action to move ourselves into a rested and relaxed state, the body will do whatever is necessary to maintain itself in a state of survival.

The second stage of stress is when the body goes into a state of resistance. If there is no response, the body forms a mechanism that learns to cope with the event, rather than resolve the situation. Yet even if it seems like the body is coping with the stressful event, its resources are gradually being drained as it does whatever is necessary to keep itself in the state of survival or preparedness.

At stage 2 you may experience:

- Feeling weak (you are an easy target for viral and bacterial illnesses, such as colds and flu)
- Being forgetful
- Anxiousness
- Drinking or smoking more
- Eating more (particularly sugary and fatty foods)
- Weariness
- Exhaustion
- Depression
- Turning to drugs (recreational or prescription)

Stage 3: EXHAUSTION

If you find yourself stuck in stage 2 and no action is taken to address it, you will eventually progress to stage 3, in which the final stage of overload and exhaustion sets in. This is when you are physically, mentally and emotionally spent. It is the point at which your bridge collapses under its excessive load.

The exhaustion stage occurs when the body has used up all its resources to cope with the stress and can no longer behave in the manner that it normally does. This is where you will start to see serious symptoms of stress and if the situation is not taken care of, stress can cause long-term damage to the body and immune system. At this stage you are likely to struggle with even basic functions of life, such as washing and getting out of bed, and many people can literally lose the will to live. It is therefore vital to catch stress at stage 1 and prevent it from ever progressing to the stage where it will have a detrimental impact on your life.

At stage 3 you may experience:

- Burnout
- Chronic fatigue
- Severe panic attacks
- Nervous breakdown
- Psychotic episodes
- Heart attack
- Suicidal thoughts or attempted suicide

WHAT HAPPENS IN THE BODY WHEN WE ARE STRESSED?

When feeling the effects of stress, the body reacts very dramatically, immediately releasing the hormone adrenaline into the bloodstream. Adrenaline increases our heart rate and blood pressure and raises our glucose levels. Cortisol, one of the hormones that provide the body with energy, is also produced. Cortisol stimulates fat and carbohydrate metabolism, creating a ready supply of energy—in the form of glucose—to prepare for a fight-or-flight situation. It is cortisol that gets our systems pumping. Once cortisol and adrenaline are in action, breathing becomes shallow and blood flows away from the skin surface to parts of the body that require more energy in an emergency—the internal organs and brain, for instance. This is one of the reasons why we might turn pale through stress and, in the long term, our skin may suffer as the nourishment it needs is being diverted to important organs. Added to this, the stomach releases more hydrochloric acid than it would normally require. Hydrochloric acid is needed to break down our food, but under stress we produce too much, which can be damaging to the stomach lining. The muscles tense to prepare to fight or flee and many internal organs—spleen, liver, brain, heart and so on—go into overdrive, working much harder than they should need to. This uses up lots of vital energy, blood supply, oxygen and nutrients—all of which are wasted.

System shutdown

Most of us, if we are required to fight or run for our lives, would use our hands, feet, arms and legs as shields and weapons. We would kick, punch, block and defend. Therefore the muscles in the arms and legs as well as some of the major organs need to be optimized and prioritized in a survival situation. As a consequence, energy (or oxygenated blood) needs to be diverted to the essential systems required for survival and drawn away from nonessential systems, which can be "temporarily" shut down.

What do we mean by "temporary"? If you are being attacked by a sabertooth tiger, how long is that situation going to last? Seconds maybe, minutes at most. If in that space of time you have not dealt with the situation, the situation has dealt with you and you have become the tiger's lunch! So what systems of your body could be shut down for a few minutes without any long-term adverse consequences? Let's look at a few key examples:

Higher brain function

What kind of decisions do you need to make if you are being attacked by a sabertooth tiger? They would, of course, be decisions related to your ability to survive the current threat that you are facing. These decisions take place in a part of the brain called the medulla oblongata. It is also known as the primitive or reptilian brain. This part of the brain's job is to keep you alive; it doesn't get involved in problem solving, lateral thinking or creative thought processes—these processes are known as higher brain function. When we are stressed, higher brain function is shut down, as it could prevent us from doing what is necessary to remove ourselves from the source of the danger. For example, there may well have been times when you have reacted under stress and later, while relaxed, you reflect on that experience. You will find that you come up with many alternative solutions to the challenge you were facing, which would have allowed you to address your challenge more effectively and efficiently. In a relaxed state we are able to think more clearly and creatively, focus and problem solve as we engage our higher brain function. So why does nature shut down higher brain function when we are stressed?

What would happen if, when faced with a sabertooth tiger, instead of turning to flee or attempting to overpower and incapacitate the tiger, you pulled out your iPad and began structuring a really great escape plan? Obviously the course of action is flawed because while you are drawing out your escape plan the tiger has been chewing your leg off! Nature, in its infinite wisdom, shuts down the parts of our brains responsible for problem solving, lateral thinking and creative thinking, as they would prevent us from acting or reacting in such a way as to save ourselves. In a life-threatening situation, action of any kind is better that inaction. Expanded, analytical and rational thought processes would prevent that action and thus could be the difference between life and death.

The problem we face in modern life is that in the kind of situations in which many of us experience stress, we do need our creative-thinking skills, our problem-solving abilities and our lateral-thinking skills to be working efficiently if we are to find the best solutions to our challenges. And most of us also will not be risking our lives if we do take a few minutes to put ourselves in the right state to find the best solutions.

Immune system

Would it help you to have your immune system functioning efficiently when being attacked by a sabertooth tiger? The immune system is obviously a very important function of the human body; however, it is not necessary for the needs of immediate survival. Have you ever come down with a cold or flu during or soon after a stressful experience? Stress suppresses the immune system, which in turn predisposes us to medical illness. You may be getting flu injections, taking vitamins and washing your hands, but practicing stress-management techniques is an important and all-natural way to stay healthy during the cold and flu season and to avoid more serious health problems year round (see Chapter 5 for more information on stress and health).

Pain

Pain is a useful and necessary reaction, even though most people would choose to avoid it where possible. If you hold your finger in a flame it will hurt, and the pain tells you that something is wrong and you need to take action to address it, which will result in you pulling your finger out. If it didn't hurt, you would hold your finger there until it burned to a cinder. However, what if your life was under threat? Would pain be an essential sensation to trigger a need to remove yourself from that situation?

This question was put into perspective for me recently while working with a soldier. He had returned from Afghanistan and was suffering from post-traumatic stress disorder. He had been on patrol and his unit had come under attack. They had radioed for air cover and for reinforcements; however, before support arrived, the battle raged. Eventually, about 30 minutes later, support did come and they were evacuated. As this young soldier was loaded into the troop carrier, his colleague made him aware that his sleeve had turned red and was dripping blood. As the medic cut his sleeve away it became clear that he had been shot. The soldier started to become hysterical. It was only a flesh wound; however, the sight of blood and torn flesh overwhelmed him. He went into shock and was then sedated. The interesting thing is that he had probably been shot between 10 and 20 minutes before he reacted to the injury, so why didn't he feel the pain at the time the injury occurred? What would the pain have prevented him from doing? If he had reacted hysterically at the time the injury occurred, it would have prevented him from continuing to fight. It could also have cost him his life or the lives of his colleagues. Being in a state of stress and thus not registering his pain served to keep him alive.

I do appreciate that many of you reading this won't live or work in a war zone, nor will you be shot at on a daily basis, but have you ever finished a long and stressful day and as you got up to go home suddenly realized that your back is aching, that you have a headache or that your shoulders are really tight? If so, really you are no different to the soldier: you shut off your pain response while under stress. Your headache may have started in the morning, your shoulders tightening up at lunchtime, your backache developing after lunch. Yet, while shutting off his pain was an appropriate response for the soldier, yours stopped you from taking action that could have prevented it from becoming a big issue at the end of the day. If you had been aware of the pain when it formed, you could have taken action to prevent it from progressing—stretched, fetched a glass of water or gone out for some fresh air.

Digestion

If you are faced with a sabertooth tiger that is preparing to pounce, will your body's ability to digest food help you in any way to deal with the challenge that you are facing? When stress activates the fight-or-flight response in your central nervous system, digestion can be shut down because your central nervous system shuts down blood flow, which affects the contractions of your digestive muscles, reducing the number of contractions they make and thus decreasing the secretions needed for digestion. As a result, stress can cause indigestion and make you feel nauseous. It can cause your colon to react in a way that gives you diarrhea or constipation.

Think of the athlete or the student who has to rush to the bathroom before the big game or exam. Stress will impact your body's ability to absorb the nutrients from your food. You may suffer from a loss of appetite and heartburn, and general stomach pains are also common.

Libido

If you are about to be pounced on by a sabertooth tiger, will your sex drive aid your survival? I am sure it is safe to say that for most people it will be the last thing on their mind. A diminished interest in sex is one of many symptoms that can develop as a result of increased psychological stress, and studies show that a decreased sex drive is a common complaint in people who have stressful jobs and work long hours.

The stress response decimates sex drive by diminishing the amount of oxygenated blood flowing to the reproductive organs, leading to issues like erectile dysfunction in men. Women are also affected, it's just more noticeable when it happens to a man. As the libido is a function that is not required for immediate survival, this is a perfectly acceptable

STRESS MAKES YOU FAT!
Does stress make you gain weight?
Science says yes.

While we tend to view stress as toxic to our minds, we generally don't always consider its potentially harmful effects on the body. As we have seen, stress causes the rocketing of many hormones—a signal to flood your cells with the energy they need, in the form of blood sugar and fat, to deal with the threat. Under stress, your body goes into fight-or-flight mode, cortisol is released and blood sugar levels are raised to prepare you for action. In the short term, the release of cortisol equips us to deal with challenging situations; however, over longer periods it is a detrimental process as it decreases our digestive ability and slows the metabolic system (the rate at which our bodies burn energy when at rest). It also prompts the release of insulin in the body, which in turn causes the body to produce glucose that it will burn as fuel to maintain itself in a state of stress and leads to an increase in appetite. Thus many people under stress find that they want to eat more, yet they become less able to burn the energy off—a double blow for those watching their waistlines.

short-term measure; however, in the long term, it will inevitably impact on relationships and lead to frustration. Men may turn to Viagra to address the symptoms; however, taking the time to relax will result in the body beginning to function normally and blood flow to the genitals returning, resulting in an increased sex drive. It is important to note that stress can also have an impact on both male and female fertility, it can affect the menstrual cycle and in some cases cause miscarriage.

The point I'm making here is that an attack by a sabertooth tiger would only last a few moments. If you survive the attack, the bodily functions that you need for everyday life—higher brain function, immune system, pain, digestion and libido—should resume working as normal. Our bodies are built to handle short periods of stress, but prolonged exposure of it can damage our normal systems, leading to physical and mental health problems.

WHAT DO YOU EXPERIENCE WHEN YOU GET STRESSED?

For most people the response to this question generally focuses on the feelings or emotions of stress:

- I feel overwhelmed
- I feel angry
- I feel frustrated
- I feel anxious
- I feel panicky
- I feel confused

The interesting thing is that stress isn't a feeling or an emotion. It is actually a physical response to internal or external stressors. There is an emotional response associated with stress; however, it is generally a side effect of the physiological changes.

The best way for me to help you understand what we experience when we get stressed is to share a personal experience with you. Many people think that, as the director of The Stress Management Society, I must never get stressed. This is a rather odd thought! Would you ask a doctor if he gets ill? Or a mechanic if his car breaks down? Of course not. We all know that doctors get ill and that mechanics' cars break down—they just know what to do when it happens. I would describe myself in the same way. I get stressed just like everyone else, yet I am able to recognize it early and do something about it.

Recently I had a scheduled business trip to The Hague. My train was leaving London at 6:19 p.m. and I knew it wouldn't take me more than 45 minutes to get to the station. To allow for any potential delays and to give me time to pick up my tickets, I left 1½ hours before my train was due to depart. I caught the Underground from my home and was merrily going about my journey when halfway through it the Underground train was held on a platform. Apparently there had been a signal failure further down the line. At first this delay didn't concern me: I had built in "buffer time" to allow for any unexpected delays. But 10 minutes passed, then 15, then 20 and still there was no movement. I was starting to cut it fine. More time passed and at this point I was going to struggle to make it. As the thought that I was going to miss my train registered, I could feel myself going into stress. My heart began pounding in my chest, my breathing became shallow and fast, my muscles tensed and I was aware I was gripping my phone in my hand more tightly. I was feeling much warmer; the temperature hadn't changed in the train but I felt beads of sweat forming on my brow. My bladder relaxed and I felt the need to pee. My teeth gritted and feelings of anger and hostility began to rise toward the idiot who caused the delay WHEN I NEEDED TO BE SOMEWHERE! My blood pressure had risen, my blood sugar had risen, my stomach was in knots and I was so angry and frustrated I failed to hear the announcement updating us on the situation.

Now, I admit I have exaggerated a little for effect, yet can you relate to these symptoms? I was experiencing a fight-or-flight response and these changes were triggered by the release of substances such as adrenaline and cortisol into my bloodstream that changed the way my body was functioning. For what reason? What was the benefit of me experiencing those changes? What did it better equip me to do? How did it help me to deal with the predicament I was facing? I needed to think of a solution to the consequence of missing my international connection, so how did this response help me to be in a state of physical preparation when I needed my mental faculties to be working efficiently? It didn't, in fact it became a counterproductive state. Unless I was planning to kick the door of the train open and run down the platform, there was nothing I could physically do to deal with the situation. And even if I had taken that course of action it probably wouldn't have been the most appropriate way of dealing with the situation. My state of stress was preventing me from finding the best solution to deal with my experience.

Fortunately for me, the train eventually moved off and there were no further delays. I arrived at my station with literally a few minutes to spare, yet I was still highly stressed as I was not sure I would be able to dash across the station in time to make my international connection. I ran as fast as I could and when I reached the platform I could hear the final announcement and the doors beeping, signifying the train was about to depart. I dived into the train and as soon as I did the doors closed behind me. What do you think was the first thing I did when I made it onto the train? (For those of you thinking I went to the bar for a drink, we will talk about why I didn't do that later in the book.) I took a deep sigh . . .

Why do we sigh after a stressful experience? Many people feel that it is the relief of the stress ending; however, the truth is much more simple. When we are stressed our breathing becomes very shallow and fast and we can begin suffocating. When the stress is over we are literally gasping for air—we need to get more oxygen into our body—so we take a long, deep breath. That needs to be released, hence the sigh when you exhale. The deepening and lengthening of your breath serves to relax you.

I had made it! I could now relax. I had used stress constructively to enable me to run to the best of my ability and catch my train. As I now relaxed, the hormones that had put me into my state of stress were dissipating, literally burned off by the physical activity.

GET TO KNOW HOW STRESS AFFECTS YOU

To get the most out of this book, it's vital to think about how stress affects your life. I'm going to ask you to create a well-being journal. You will use it throughout the book to log your responses to the exercises as well as track your progress. Start by answering the following questions in your journal:

1) What does stress mean to you?
2) What is the cause of stress to you in your life?
3) How does it affect you:
   a) Physically?
   b) Emotionally?
4) How often?
5) How have you been dealing with it until now?
6) How could you deal with it?

RELAXATION

We have already established what happens to your body when you're stressed and in fight-or-flight mode, but what happens when we are relaxed? Being in a relaxed and rested state brings all sorts of physical and psychological benefits. For example, you experience:

- A decreased heart rate (improved cardiac function)
- Slow and deep breathing (more oxygen enters your body so it works efficiently)
- Normal function of blood vessels and circulation
- Normal saliva function (aids digestion)
- Inhibited production of white blood cells (improved immune response)
- Relaxed muscles
- Reduced blood pressure
- Reduced blood sugar (leading to stable eating patterns)
- Normal function of the sweat glands
- Normal digestion
- Restful and calm feelings

Remember it is physically impossible to be anxious and relaxed at the same time.

CHAPTER 3

THE SLAVERY OF STRESS

In today's world, so many of us are operating from a state of survival. We're concerned with staying alive, keeping a roof over our heads and food on our plates. We're rarely concerned by issues beyond ourselves and we don't have the capacity to care about the economy or the climate because we are all so busy dealing with the challenges of our day-to-day life. We live a highly consumerist lifestyle—new technologies and fashions constantly tempt us—and money needs to be earned to pay for us to maintain this lifestyle. We have bills to pay and many of us have debts: credit card bills, loans and mortgages. We are indentured slaves to the stress of these problems, struggling to buy a freedom that we may never achieve. That said, and as this chapter will show, there are times when stress *can* be of use to us; we simply need to work out when and how to use it positively, and how to realize when it is having a negative impact on our lives—when we are becoming its slave—and how to remove ourselves from that situation.

POSITIVE AND NEGATIVE USES OF STRESS

As we have already established, stress is a physical response, designed to equip you to do whatever is necessary either to fight your way out of danger or to remove yourself from the cause of the stress. In modern life, there are examples of how we can use that stress constructively and many situations in which we experience stress but it is a counter-productive response.

How can stress help you?

Even though stress has been demonized in modern society, being branded as the cause of all our problems, I just want to make my position clear: I do not think stress is a bad thing nor do I think stress is the problem. In fact, my belief is that stress can be a good thing. Nature gave us stress for a very good reason and if used appropriately it can literally be the difference between life and death. If it wasn't for stress you wouldn't be reading this book, nor would I have written it, because our species would have become extinct many thousands of years ago. Stress was the response that allowed early humans not only to survive all the challenges that they faced but also to thrive. Getting stressed is not the problem; the problem is getting stressed in situations in which it is not the most appropriate response. In certain situations a degree of stress can be useful to focus and sharpen our minds so that we achieve a desired outcome:

- Anyone who has to perform for a living—from professional athletes to singers and actors—will tell you that stress can pump them up and get them ready for action. It's when it gets too great that it becomes a problem.
- If you were faced with an emergency situation like finding yourself in a burning building, stress would equip you to do what is necessary to escape.
- Stress can even be useful when running for a bus or a train, spurring you on to run faster to catch it.
- If you were driving on the highway and someone started veering into your lane, stress would be very useful in enabling you to take action very rapidly—either to slam on the brakes or to steer out of the way.

There is an urban legend that a frail old lady was walking with her grandson one wintery day. She had a back problem and walked with the aid of a walking stick. A teenager driving down the street lost control of her vehicle and came skidding off the road. In the confusion the old lady and her grandson became separated and the child was crushed by the vehicle. The distraught grandmother came rushing over to find her beloved grandson pinned underneath the car and as the story goes she was able to lift the vehicle off the child so he could be removed to safety.

Could this really be possible? I believe it absolutely is. Remarkable things have been done by people who get so emotionally charged that the adrenaline shoots through their body, allowing them to have almost impossible strength. Although I would imagine that the grandmother's body would feel some repercussions the following day, I do believe the endangered life of her grandchild could create enough adrenaline to enable her to lift a car off him.

So as you can see, stress can be a positive motivating force. Why would Caveman Joe ever have left the warmth, comfort and safety of his cave if he weren't stressed or concerned about his family starving to death if he didn't leave it to hunt or forage for food?

HOW MIGHT STRESS BE A HINDRANCE TO YOU?

There are many situations in which we experience stress and it is not a helpful response; in fact, it impacts negatively on the situation and our ability to deal with it. Examples could include:

- Being stuck in a traffic jam
- Your computer crashing
- Taking an exam

- A job interview
- Getting married

In these examples, there is nothing to fight or run away from, so getting stressed simply ends up preventing us from functioning at our best. You have gone into a state of physical preparation in which your higher brain function and other essential systems have shut down (see pages 17–23) yet there is no physical action to take. This state then becomes counterproductive, preventing you from thinking clearly, making good decisions and finding the best solutions.

HOW VULNERABLE ARE YOU TO STRESS?

Take a few minutes to understand how vulnerable you are to stress. Mark each of the statements below from 0 (always applies to you) to 5 (never applies to you), according to how accurate each statement is in describing your current lifestyle.

1) I eat at least one balanced meal a day.
2) I get seven to eight hours of sleep at least four nights a week.
3) I have at least one person who lives nearby of whom I can ask a favor.
4) I exercise to the point of perspiration at least twice a week.
5) I do not smoke.
6) I drink fewer than five alcoholic drinks a week.
7) I am the appropriate weight for my height.
8) I drink fewer than two cups of coffee (or tea, or cola) every day.
9) I have a network of friends, family and acquaintances on whom I can rely.
10) I confide with at least one person in my network about personal matters.

11) I am generally in good health.

12) I am able to speak openly about my feelings when angry, stressed or worried.

13) I do something for fun at least once a week.

14) I recognize stress symptoms.

15) I take quiet time for myself during the day.

16) I have an income adequate to meet my basic expenses.

17) I spend less than an hour each day traveling to and from work.

18) I am calm when I am kept waiting/stuck in traffic/late for an appointment.

19) I have regular calm conversations with the people I live with about domestic problems, such as chores, money and daily living issues.

20) I never try to do everything myself.

21) I never race through a day.

22) I never complain about time wasted and the past.

23) I feel organized and in control.

24) I am able to organize my time effectively.

25) I recognize when I am not coping well under pressure.

Add up your scores. If you scored:

Over 80: EMERGENCY!

This score indicates that you are experiencing damaging amounts of stress that if left unchecked will seriously affect your health, relationships and work efficiency. You potentially have a lot of stress in your life but few mechanisms to help you cope with it, so you need this book urgently. You need to take charge of your lifestyle now by following my 10-step stress solution. Read on to find out how to change your attitudes and pay careful attention to your diet, exercise and relaxation. Learn to prioritize, delegate and to say no.

Finish absorbing the valuable information in this book, and if you feel you still need to seek further help:

- See a counselor (http://www.stress.org.uk/personal-consultation.aspx)
- Visit The Stress Management Society free factsheets area (http://www.stress.org.uk/fact-sheets.aspx) and download the various free books and resources to give you the support you need.
- Attend a workshop on stress management.
- Attend a local yoga class or have a massage.
- This may be a good opportunity to take a break and get some much needed rest and relaxation!

50–79: You are approaching the danger zone.

This score indicates that there are times when your life becomes extremely stressful. You have a vulnerability to stress, and the higher your score the more serious the problem is. You may well be suffering stress-related symptoms, your relationships may be strained and you may not be operating in your most resourceful state. Read on to find out how the 10-step stress solution will be of huge benefit to you: it will help you to look at your lifestyle and identify what things cause you stress and then work out how to reduce their impact.

25–49: You are in fairly good control of your life.

This is an average score and indicates normal levels of stress, but your score indicates that you do still have a vulnerability to stress. Your lifestyle is such that your body's "shock absorbers" can deal with stress in a healthy, nonaggressive way. Even so, watch out for potential hot spots. Work on the choices and habits that could still be causing you some unnecessary stress in your life. Seek alternative ways to complete tasks that are currently causing stress or anxiety.

0–24: Congratulations! You are a calm and relaxed individual.

You seem to enjoy a good lifestyle. There seem to be few hassles in your life and you do not seem vulnerable to stress. Your lifestyle is such that stress has a minimal impact on your well-being. You are managing your lifestyle effectively and efficiently. Make sure, though, that you are not trying so hard to avoid problems that you are shying away from challenges. Listen to your body. When you are tired, hungry or thirsty, do something about it. Also recognize stress and anger in your day and counter it immediately with a brisk walk, 10 minutes in deep relaxation or whatever works for you.

CHAPTER 4

COPING WITH STRESS

What do you do when you get stressed? What is it that you usually turn to to alleviate the symptoms of stress? What are your coping mechanisms? Think back to the questionnaire in Chapter 2 on page 26: How did you respond to question 5 (on how you deal with stress)?

The Stress Management Society conducted a study whereby we asked people to complete the statement "I'm so stressed I need a . . ." to see what people were likely to turn to to make themselves feel better during periods of stress. How would you complete that statement? What do you think might have been the top four answers?

In no particular order, the top four things that people are most likely to reach for are:

1) Alcohol
2) Cigarettes
3) Caffeine
4) Refined sugar (cookies, cakes, candies, chocolate, etc.)

All of these substances are stimulants (although see the following page for an explanation of why alcohol is also a depressant) and cannot possibly calm you down. Let us return to our example of Caveman Joe and the sabertooth tiger from Chapter 1. Imagine that just as Joe is about to be pounced on by the tiger we are able to freeze the tiger in midair. We then give Joe three alcoholic drinks, get him to eat five chocolate bars, smoke 10 cigarettes and knock back four espressos. Now let's unfreeze the tiger. Is Caveman Joe now relaxed? Of course not. In fact, I believe that he would be so stimulated that the tiger is highly likely to lose the battle and end up as a rug on the cave floor. That is obviously a highly exaggerated scenario; and it is unlikely that anyone is going to consume all of those things when stressed; however, the point is that the stimulants we reach for to *alleviate* stress actually have the reverse effect than the one we are looking for. So why is it that as rational, intelligent adults we turn to substances that we know cannot possibly give us the long-term solutions we are looking for?

Before we go on to look at why we crave these stimulants, let's have a look at what effects these substances have on our bodies.

ALCOHOL

I often get criticized for describing alcohol as a stimulant. In the drugs pantheon, alcohol is classed as a depressant, along with barbiturates, tranquilizers and anesthetics. However, alcohol is a biphasic substance, which means it has two phases, or effects, depending on the quantity consumed. If consumed in low quantities it acts as a mild stimulant. As concentrations in the bloodstream increase, stimulation gives way to sedation, then stupor, coma and finally death. The excitement phase is characterized by exhilaration, loss of restraint and inhibitions, increased confidence, talkativeness, mood swings and displays of extreme emotion. Physical symptoms include slurred speech, sensory disturbance—increased tolerance to pain, for example—poor balance and impaired judgment. Most people display this kind of functional depression with blood alcohol concentrations at or below 0.1 percent. By 0.3 percent, all but the most hardened drinkers are visibly drunk, and by 0.4 percent, most people would be asleep. At higher levels, coma sets in, with the risk of death through numbing of the heart or the breathing section of the brain. As most of us would consume smaller quantities of alcohol to deal with a stressful day, it is highly likely to have a stimulating effect.

Alcohol also has secondary negative effects on the body and on our ability to deal with stress, in the form of the "hangover" we feel after excessive drinking. Common characteristics of a hangover include a headache, nausea, sensitivity to light and noise, lethargy, diarrhea and thirst, typically after the intoxicating effect of the alcohol begins to wear off. In addition to the physical symptoms, a hangover may also induce psychological symptoms including heightened feelings of stress, depression and anxiety.

CIGARETTES

Cigarettes contain more than 4,000 chemical compounds and at least 400 toxic substances. The general term used to describe these toxins is "tar," which in its solid form is the brown, sticky substance that you can see on the end of a cigarette filter. Tar is thought to be the substance associated with an increased risk of lung cancer. Aside from the harm it alone causes, perhaps the most dangerous component in cigarettes is nicotine—the colorless, flavorless, poisonous and highly addictive chemical that is what makes us reach for more of the tar.

When nicotine is inhaled or absorbed, it enters the bloodstream and is quickly sent to the brain. Once there, it causes temporary sensations of pleasure, satisfaction and reward; however, these effects wear off very quickly and over time your body develops tolerance to these effects and requires increasingly higher levels of nicotine in order to regain those feelings of pleasure. The result? Your brain tells your body to keep supplying nicotine, and when it doesn't get it fast enough, nicotine cravings kick in. Ready for the truth? While many people may feel they are using cigarettes as a way to relax or de-stress, nicotine actually causes the opposite effect. Studies have found that nicotine intensifies stress. Feelings of calmness or pleasure during tobacco use are really just momentary reliefs from the unpleasant effects (including stress) that come along with nicotine cravings. Those feelings of stress and anxiety will return once the nicotine leaves their system and the cycle begins again.

When heavy smokers—addicts—don't smoke for a while, they may start to experience nicotine withdrawal. Symptoms can range from physical ailments, including chronic disorders such as high blood pressure and impotence, to psychological ones, such as anxiety. If you experience anxiety, nervousness and irritability when you haven't had your regular cigarette, you may think other things in your life are causing you to feel this way. So, when you smoke, you alleviate some of the nicotine withdrawal symptoms and then believe that it's the nicotine that has calmed your nerves. You may not realize the power of your mind to calm your body's reaction to stress. As a smoker, you have convinced yourself that nicotine relieves stress; however, it's not the drug itself but your *belief* that it is.

Similarly, the act of smoking is actually a breathing relaxation technique. When you smoke, you inhale and exhale, and may even do it rhythmically. Many people who do not smoke often use this breathing relaxation technique to manage their stress without consuming nicotine. In many parts of the USA and Europe you can no longer smoke indoors, so if you are at work you have to go outside to smoke. This gives you a break and removes you from the source of your stress; the walk outside may give you a little physical activity. While you are outside you get some fresh air and the deep drags on your cigarette not only fill your lungs with smoke, they give you some extra oxygen too.

What I am trying to illustrate is that the smoker gets a host of benefits that have nothing to do with the cigarette itself. You could have gone outside and sucked on a plastic straw and experienced the same benefit—and have plenty more money in your pocket! So rather than going for a cigarette break, go for a fresh-air break! This book features many effective ways to manage stress, and by quitting tobacco you can break the cycle and eliminate the stress caused by nicotine addiction.

CAFFEINE

Caffeine is a highly popular pick-me-up used to raise energy levels, or to keep us awake longer than our body wants to be. It is another stimulant, and a common misconception is that it gives you a boost in energy. Caffeine does not increase your energy levels, it provides only a chemical stimulation to your body. You may experience a brief "perceived" boost in energy as the tea, coffee, cola or energy drink boosts the positive messengers in your brain, but you will then suffer the side effects of such an induced state, including fatigue and irritability as your energy levels actually fall.

In England, tea is the liquid that lubricates society. There is no problem that cannot be solved by putting the kettle on. My colleague Simran can make up to a dozen cups of tea in a day, many of which never get drunk. She just finds the process of getting up from whatever she is doing, boiling the kettle and making her cup of tea relaxing. And, globally, the concept of coffee culture dates back centuries, with coffee shops long having been recognized as places of social gathering. We often even refer to a break as a tea or coffee break.

If you ingest high levels of caffeine, you may feel your mood soar and plummet, leaving you craving more caffeine to make it soar again. Although it can give you a quick boost when required, the fatigue will catch up once the caffeine has worn off. You should not need caffeine to focus, and if you do, this lack of focus is your body's way of telling you it needs rest. An excess of caffeine can lead to negative effects such as restlessness, lapses of concentration and a decrease in your ability to be fully effective. Caffeine also has a massive impact on the hormones in your body. The following hormones are increased under the influence of caffeine:

- **Adenosine:** keeps you alert but causes sleep problems in the future.
- **Adrenaline:** gives you a boost but will make you feel fatigued once the adrenaline has worn off.
- **Cortisol:** the stress hormone.
- **Dopamine:** initially makes you feel happy but once worn off, generates a low and possible dependence/addiction.

Even moderate caffeine consumption will make you feel like you are having a stressful day. And because caffeine *and* stress can both elevate cortisol levels, high amounts of caffeine (or stress) can lead to the negative health effects associated with prolonged elevated levels of cortisol, such as erratic or complete loss of sleep, impaired cognitive performance, high blood pressure, lowered immunity and, of course, you feel more stressed. In the long term, if you combine this with additional work pressures, it can increase blood pressure significantly, leading to an increased risk of long-term heart disease.

REFINED SUGAR

Chocolates, cookies, cakes, candies, sodas and other carbohydrate and sugar-rich foods are common sources of comfort when we are under pressure. Sugar is rapidly absorbed into the bloodstream, so you get a sudden rise in blood sugar (glucose) levels that brings an immediate boost to the positive messengers. It's why we reach for a sugary snack, chocolate bar or cookie when we are feeling low.

The human body burns two things as fuel—fat and sugar. Both of these fuels have distinctly different properties. Put a flame to sugar at room temperature and it will ignite very quickly; however, it will not burn for very long at all. Put a flame to fat or oil at room temperature and nothing happens; for the fat to burn, the temperature must be raised. When it is hot enough it will eventually ignite and when it does it will burn for ages and ages. So which is the more sustainable fuel source? Fat. However, if you were being attacked by a sabertooth tiger, sugar would in fact be the best fuel source because you need it quickly and only for a short period. So in an emergency or life-threatening situation, going into a sugar-burning state is a perfectly appropriate response. The human body has stores of both sugar and fat. At any one time we have stored, on average, approximately 2,500 calories worth of sugar compared with a whopping 160,000 calories worth of usable fat. Fat was intended to be our primary fuel source, but sugar is the fuel of choice when operating from a state of stress.

However, the effects are only a temporary fix because they are always followed by a rapid fall in the sugar levels. This sets off a vicious cycle where you keep consuming more sugar to avoid the crash feeling. This is not something that is beneficial in terms of rebalancing your body and is at best only a short-term solution. Likewise, high levels of stress can stimulate the rapid release of cortisol, which can further exacerbate higher blood sugar levels. So it stands to reason that a rise in blood sugar would tend to produce anxiety.

WHY DOES THE BODY CRAVE STIMULANTS WHEN STRESSED?

In using stimulants, all we are looking for is a temporary solution to alleviate the symptoms; a quick fix, a magic pill. Even though none of these substances can possibly calm you down, using them may leave you feeling relaxed (or at least less stressed) and they will temporarily increase the sense of "feeling good" that we usually get from our own positive brain messengers—adrenaline, serotonin and dopamine. So if you have your breakfast at 7:00 a.m., get stuck in a traffic jam on the way to work, arrive late for a meeting, discover your laptop has blown up and with it the presentation you have been working on for the last two weeks, by about 11:00 a.m. you will be feeling drained and exhausted by stress. You will probably be craving that cup of coffee, chocolate bar, energy drink, or even worse, cigarette or shot of tequila under the illusion that it will calm you down! If you were to consume one of these substances, you would magically feel recharged and ready to go again, correct? Well, if you do feel a sense of relief it is not because they relaxed you or removed your stress; it is because they are literally fuel for your stress: they simply filled up the tank to allow you to feel stressed for a little longer.

One thing that is noticeable about using external stimulants to change our brain chemistry is that they are rarely used in isolation. We turn to all kinds of solutions like tobacco, alcohol, sugar and caffeine to help us boost the number of positive messengers getting through to our brain. However, you cannot accurately rebalance your brain messengers in this way. Your body needs to make this delicate chemical adjustment itself, and if you are serious about wanting to reduce stress, then you need to dramatically reduce, or avoid, all of these stimulants. Don't get me wrong—I, like many people, will on occasion enjoy a nice meal with friends with maybe a glass or two of wine, possibly some chocolate pudding for dessert and a cup of tea to finish. The difference is that I was relaxed when I started the meal; I did not turn to the stimulants to relax. Rather than turn to them when you are stressed, do something to relax first, and then if you still desire the cup of coffee or the chocolate bar then at least you are not turning to it to achieve a result that it cannot possibly give you. For many of us it is the break that using these substances gives us that relieves our stress; however, we do not need to consume anything to get the break.

The best strategies to deal with stress don't cost anything, don't require consuming anything, nor do they have any side effects. Because they have no real commercial value you would probably not even have heard of many of them. That is why I developed the 10-step stress solution, to empower you to tackle stress when it occurs without using the flawed strategies that simply do not give us the results we are looking for.

The only way to cope when you have too much stress, when your bridge is bowing and buckling under excessive load, is to:

1) Strengthen your bridge by getting extra support or
2) Lighten the load by having less pressure (less work and fewer tasks)

It is not always possible to lighten your load, so my 10-step stress solution is designed to give you more support so that you are better equipped to cope with the stresses and demands with which life will inevitably burden you. Following each of these 10 steps will equip you with a toolbox of techniques to make your bridge stronger—strong enough to cope with the ever increasing demands of modern life without you turning to the coping mechanisms, such as stimulants, that you might believe strengthen you against stress, but in fact only cause your bridge to buckle even further. Turn the page to begin building a strong bridge.

PART 2
THE 10-STEP STRESS SOLUTION

CHAPTER 5

STEP 1:
Prioritize your health

Many people aren't tuned in to their body and aren't aware, until it's too late, of the effects that stress is having on them. So in order to assess your state of health, answer the questions below.

ASSESS YOUR HEALTH

Do you find you are prone to illness during or after periods of stress?   Y/N

If a cold or a flu is going around are you the first one to catch it?   Y/N

Does it take longer than normal for you to recover from illness?   Y/N

Do you have a serious or long-term health condition?   Y/N

Do you frequently feel these symptoms at the same time: abdominal pain, bloating and feeling full very quickly? Y/N

Are you a smoker or do you live with one?   Y/N

Have you recently gained weight or lost weight for no apparent reason?   Y/N

If you answered yes to all or most of those questions, you need some help. This chapter will give you a great start, with many practical suggestions on improving your health and well-being.

WHAT'S THE LINK BETWEEN STRESS AND POOR HEALTH?

The physical effects of stress on the human body are well documented: when your mind is not functioning optimally or is plagued by negative thoughts and emotions, eventually your body will suffer the consequences. Stress undoubtedly makes people ill. Indeed, the top four killers on the planet have been linked to stress (heart disease, cancer, stroke and adult-onset type-2 diabetes). In addition, stress is now known to contribute to hypertension and high blood pressure, digestive conditions such as IBS (irritable bowel syndrome), asthma, chronic pain, various skin disorders, accidents, suicide, depression, ulcers, muscle and joint pain, miscarriage, allergies, alopecia (spontaneous hair loss), premature tooth loss and other conditions. The effect of stress on the immune system and the functioning of the body in general has clearly linked it to poor health and death, and Harvard researchers estimate that 60–90 percent of doctors' visits are caused by stress. Let's look at a few key examples of the links between stress and poor health.

Stress and the heart (cardiovascular system)

The function of the circulatory (or cardiovascular) system is to transport gases, such as oxygen, and hormones around the body, plus to transport nutrients to your cells and waste from your cells. The heart is the pump that powers the circulatory system, so if the circulation is poor the heart has to work harder to pump the blood, putting it under strain and potentially leading to ailments. Other functions of the system include fighting infections and maintaining heat for your body.

Stress affects your cardiovascular system by increasing your heart rate and speeding up blood flow, which in turn can increase blood pressure (see more on this below). Eventually the physiological impact of stress will have a detrimental effect on your cardiovascular system:

- As a result of your heart rate increasing, there is a chance that your heart could develop an abnormal rhythm or the heart muscle itself could be damaged.
- Your arteries may thicken with plaque, which could cause heart disease or a heart attack. This is as a result of cholesterol and triglycerides in your bloodstream.
- An increase in your blood pressure can lead to a host of hypertension-related issues such as stroke and heart disease.
- Stress has an impact on our behavior. People who are under chronic stress are far more likely to take up smoking, drink alcohol and abuse drugs (these include pharmaceutical and recreational substances), or they may suffer from eating disorders (such as overeating or anorexia/bulimia). All of these behaviors contribute to the development of heart disease.

High blood pressure

Experiencing a stressful situation will cause a temporary spike in your blood pressure; however, can this cause hypertension (or long-term high blood pressure)? Is it possible that lots of stressful experiences that cause blood pressure spikes accumulate and cause hypertension? There is no clear-cut evidence that stress directly causes hypertension; however, it is highly likely that stress-related behaviors (such as overeating, poor diet, excessive alcohol consumption, poor sleep habits, etc.) lead to high blood pressure.

You are also very likely to suffer from palpitations or high blood pressure if you are the kind of person who reacts in an extreme way to everyday stress by blowing your top, for example, or having a tearful outburst. Even common emotions such as anger, frustration, anxiety and sadness trigger abnormal functioning of the heart and can cause permanent damage; in fact, medical research suggests that over time extreme emotions may cause damage to the heart and the coronary arteries. Studies have shown that negative emotions cause an inadequate flow of blood to the heart, which increases the risk of a heart attack.

Circulation

When you experience stress, your body restricts your blood vessels, which will prevent the blood from flowing effectively. This is how stress can cause poor circulation. Circulatory issues can cause hands and feet to become extremely cold.

Stress and digestion

When severely stressed, your body restricts blood supply to the stomach, preventing your digestive system from functioning normally. It is also important to note that the whole of the intestine is in part controlled by the nervous system, which responds to external as well as internal stimuli—including stress.

Long-term stress can lead to digestive disorders such as IBS (irritable bowel syndrome) or ulcers, and if you have preexisting conditions, stress can make the symptoms worse.

HEALTH VS FITNESS

Health and fitness are terms that are used interchangeably; however, it is important to note that there are fundamental differences between them.

Health can be described as the general condition of the body or mind—a reference to a person's overall status. This can include physical, mental, emotional, psychological and spiritual—the holistic (whole person) health of an individual. It refers to every aspect of you, your physical body and state of mind. Good health suggests being free from disease, illness or ailments and not suffering from pain. It's meaning is very loose and nonspecific; however, it does not necessarily mean that you are fit.

Fitness is not a measure of well-being, it is more a gauge of how much physical activity you are capable of. Health is not always completely within our control; however, fitness is entirely—we all have the capacity to improve our fitness by taking up relevant exercise programs. There are many ways to improve fitness—any form of vigorous cardiovascular exercise, including running, swimming or cycling. The more you exercise, the more your fitness improves. However, be aware that overdoing it can be counterproductive, leading to injury or illness. Rather than pushing yourself to the limit, it's better to steadily increase the amount of activity. When I started training for the marathon I didn't run 26.2 miles on my first run—in fact my first one was just over a mile, and with regular increases to the length of my runs, in a short time I was up to running 12–15 miles regularly. Small, incremental increases to your exercise routine will gradually (and healthily) increase your fitness. The added benefits of increased fitness will boost health in a variety of different ways, including a reduction in the risk of heart disease and many forms of cancer, and even result in a more effective immune system.

It is vital that we understand the fundamental differences between health and fitness, as the two do not necessarily go hand in hand. Many athletes get ill or are injured more than the average person and recently there have been many high-profile cases of professional sportspeople dying while competing. Even though we accept that injury is part of the game, we are shocked when a fit young sports professional drops dead on the field of play. This is where we are clear that fitness doesn't guarantee health and vice versa. For example, in football, knee, ankle and hamstring injuries are seen as "normal" wear and tear—occupational hazards of the job. However, when injuries occur to different parts of the body, such as the heart—as recently experienced by Fabrice Muamba of Bolton Wanderers in a FA Cup game against Tottenham Hotspur—we are shown that there is nothing normal about a fit, 24-year-old professional soccer player suffering from cardiac arrest, and people were perplexed.

There is a widespread belief that professional athletes are the healthiest people in society, and this is why there is such confusion when a young, seemingly healthy soccer player suffers cardiac arrest midgame. Sports professionals of all ages who suffer heart attacks and other similar problems are evidently very fit, but obviously not as healthy as they could be. Most sportspeople—both professionals and weekend warriors such as myself—invest much of our time getting fit; however, we do not seem to pursue our health with the same passion. Sadly, some people may even become less healthy due to constantly pushing their bodies beyond the limit. These kinds of health problems indicate an imbalance between a person's health and their fitness. It's important to bear in mind that you can have good health and achieve very high levels of sports performance, and you can also be extremely healthy without being particularly fit. This is a lesson I have learned firsthand as the box on the next page shows.

Take this time to commit yourself to improving your health by addressing any stressors present in your life (see page 13 for a reminder of what I mean by "stressors"). Identify areas of concern that can be easily addressed and areas that might take more time to fix. Solutions to fight stress are the same as strategies to promote good health. They involve finding techniques to boost the strength and structural integrity of your bridge to better equip you to cope with the relentless and sometimes conflicting demands of modern life. These could include:

CASE STUDY:
Neil Shah, amateur marathon runner

I learned firsthand the difference between health and fitness the first couple of times I ran a marathon. All my emphasis was on fitness, training and physical preparation and I found I had no time to invest in my health and well-being. As a result I endured significant stress from my training regime—I didn't have time to ensure I was eating the right things, possibly I overtrained and I had little time for relaxation and recovery as I still had a busy career to manage. My health suffered. During my training I caught several colds, flu and a persistent cough that I couldn't shake, and I had other niggling problems that weren't enough to stop me training, but were enough to suggest my health was suffering. On race day itself I suffered a severely injured knee.

At the time, I spoke to several other seasoned long-distance runners and was dismayed to learn that these kinds of issues are common (if not typical) for people training for a marathon. It wasn't until my second marathon, and after I'd read a book entitled *Slow Burn* by Stu Mittleman, that I realized that even though recurrent health problems and injuries may be considered to be part of training, they are not part of *healthy* training.

When I started prioritizing my health, spending time relaxing, sleeping well, incorporating yoga and meditation into my training and adopting a healthy diet, my training experience changed massively. No injuries. No colds or flu and a race completed in less than five hours. Success!

- A healthy diet (see Chapter 9)
- Exercise—either vigorous or a simple walk in the park (see Chapter 10)
- Getting a good night's sleep (see Chapter 6)
- Meditation (see Chapter 7)
- Mastering technology (see Chapter 13)
- Learning to say no (see Chapter 14)
- Doing the things you love
- Making time for yourself
- Addressing or removing unhealthy relationships
- Taking time off from work
- Reading something uplifting
- Going on vacation
- Avoiding the news for a while
- Spending time outdoors
- Managing your time more effectively
- Talking to someone and sharing your concerns

It is important to have a comprehensive understanding of your mind, body and spirit. It is also important to know how to protect your mind and body from stress and the damage it causes. Stress is a leading cause of poor health and it is up to you to reduce and, where possible, remove any stressors in your life. To help you determine how you can improve your health, complete a personal action plan by filling in the box on the next page.

MY PERSONAL ACTION PLAN

I promise myself I am going to improve my health by taking these actions:

1. _____

2. _____

3. _____

4. _____

5. _____

Enter your actions here or create a well-being journal to log your actions and progress.

CHAPTER 6

STEP 2:

Get a good night's sleep

For many people, sleep is one of the first things to suffer when they are feeling stressed. Use the questionnaire below to determine whether you are getting the best night's sleep you can.

ASSESS YOUR SLEEP

Do you find it easy to get to sleep and stay asleep?   Y/N

Do you get an average of 7–9 hours of sleep per night?   Y/N

Do you dream?   Y/N

Do you wake up naturally without an alarm?   Y/N

Is your bedroom clear of TVs, PCs and cell phones? Y/N

Is your room completely dark?   Y/N

If you answered no to all or most of those questions, you need some help. This chapter will give you a great start, with many practical suggestions on improving your bedtime routine and getting enough rest.

SLEEP: NATURE'S HEALER

Sleep is essential to maintain good mental and physical health. It is nature's healer; the opportunity for your brain and body to repair themselves from the stresses of the day and to build and develop for the future. Yet more than 50 percent of adults have insomnia a few nights a week and 25 percent suffer from insomnia most nights, lasting a month or longer. What is your day like if you have had a poor night's sleep? Do you find yourself snappy and irritable, overreacting to the most minuscule challenge? What about days when you have slept well? Are you more likely to take things in stride and stay calm under pressure? Think about the amount of sleep you are getting. Have you ever slept for 11 hours and woken up feeling exhausted? On the other hand, have you ever slept for five or six hours and woken up feeling rested and refreshed? It's not the amount of sleep that we get that determines how rested we feel, it's the depth and quality of our sleep that is important.

Understanding the different types of sleep

Not all sleep is the same. In fact there are five different stages:

- **Stage 1 (very light sleep):** the transition period between being awake and asleep; you are barely dozing.
- **Stage 2 (light sleep):** a period of rapid brain activity in which body temperature also decreases and your heartbeat slows.
- **Stage 3 (transitional sleep):** the period between light and deep sleep where your brain begins to experience the deeper, slower delta brain waves.
- **Stage 4 (deep sleep or delta sleep):** the delta brain waves are now dominating; you are hard to rouse and very groggy if woken.
- **Stage 5 (REM or rapid eye movement sleep):** your brain becomes more active and you dream but the body relaxes; this is the stage where your body repairs itself.

Most stressed people only ever achieve stages 1 and 2 and wake up feeling like they haven't had a proper rest. But if you want to be ready for the day you really need consistent deep sleep, particularly at stages 4 and 5. If you don't achieve this quantity and quality of sleep, then everything in your body is affected, from your energy levels and your mood, to your weight.

Five ways in which sleep will improve your health and well-being

1) You'll be ill less frequently

There is a clear link between sleep, your immune system and your ability to fight off infection. Study after study shows that if you skimp on rest, you are more likely to get ill. In turn, if you get enough sleep, then you create the optimum environment for your natural defenses to function well.

2) You'll be more relaxed

Get enough sleep and you'll cope better with the pressures of the day. You'll help yourself avoid building up high levels of the stress hormones cortisol and adrenaline. Both these substances put your body on high alert, watching for danger. When they are present, you are unlikely to achieve a good-quality deep sleep and will have to make do with the lower quality stage 1 or 2 sleep instead.

3) You'll regulate your weight

Many studies show a link between obesity and sleep. Your body needs sleep to normalize weight-control hormones. One study showed that those who slept for four hours two nights running had an 18 percent decrease in leptin (a hormone that gives a feeling of fullness after eating) and a 28 percent increase in ghrelin (one that makes you feel more hungry). They also had a 24 percent increase in appetite, craved sweet, starchy and salty foods and lost interest in fruit, vegetables, protein and dairy products.

4) You'll increase body strength

To build muscle you need stage 4 and 5 sleep. It is during this phase of deep sleep that the body repairs muscles that have been

CASE STUDY:
Janette Watkins—how I lost over 66 pounds in one year, in my sleep!

When I became dieter of the year at my weight loss club, it wasn't just because of good diet. It also came down to me getting enough sleep for the first time in years.

I knew that with inadequate sleep I tended to get more emotional over things and be more likely to comfort eat. So I decided to sleep more by getting to bed regularly for eight hours every night.

The results were good: I became less emotional and more logical. For example, if someone had ignored me at work, I'd have worried that he was upset or angry with me and then perhaps I'd turn to chocolate to make myself feel better. With more sleep, I could make better judgments about things like that. I could see that perhaps my colleague was pretty busy on a project and that saying "hello" to me in the cafeteria wasn't high on his list of priorities.

I also noticed that with more sleep in my life I wanted to snack less and was better able to judge when I was full. It was almost like someone flicked a switch in my head that helped me make better decisions about food.

torn or broken during the day. It's also essential for those wanting to improve muscle tone. Working out is only part of the story. The body actually waits until deep-level sleep to transform that physical activity into new muscle. So exercise without sleep is a waste of time.

5) **You'll improve your memory**
Deep sleep dramatically improves how your brain works. It affects how nerve cells in the brain connect, governing everything from how the brain controls behavior to the ability to learn or remember.

HOW MUCH SLEEP DO I NEED?

Our sleep needs change at different times of life. Babies need a lot of time asleep, whereas those of retirement age may find they don't need so much time resting. Therefore discovering how much sleep is right for you is a question of trial and error, depending on your stage of life. Margaret Thatcher famously claimed to get by on five hours per night, but different people need different amounts. Eight hours is a good starting point. It works for a large number of people, and once you start getting this amount of sleep regularly, you can work out if you need less or more.

How can I tell if I'm getting enough sleep?

You should be dreaming. Dreaming is a great sleep barometer as most people only achieve this state when their brain is deeply relaxed. Therefore if you're achieving the right amount of sleep, you will probably be dreaming most nights, even if you don't remember them upon waking. There are now gadgets and apps, such as Dream:ON, that allow you to track your sleep and monitor how much time you spend in the REM phase if you want to find out for sure.

What time should I go to bed?

It is important to get to bed at a reasonable hour. Our day is governed according to precise cycles influenced by the rotation of the earth, sun and moon. The sun rises and sets daily, and the function of sleeping and wakefulness is part of this natural rhythm. Prior to the widespread use of electricity, people would go to bed shortly after sunset, as most animals do. Thus, research shows that the best hours of sleep for your body are the hours of 10:00 p.m.–6:00 a.m. Start your eight hours later, for example at 2:00 a.m., and the depth and quality of sleep and its ability to rejuvenate the body would be severely affected. You might get the same amount of sleep, but the quality would not be as good as had you started at 10:00 p.m.

WHAT NIGHT IS BEST FOR SLEEP?

Research shows that most people with sleep problems are most likely to have trouble sleeping on a Sunday night. A study of 3,500 adults found nearly 60 percent of workers have their worst night's sleep on a Sunday and that over 25 percent call in sick the next day. By comparison around 80 percent of people have their best night's sleep on a Friday night at the end of the working week.

HOW TO IMPROVE YOUR SLEEP

The 21st century places more demands on time than ever before. Lives move at great velocity and we find ourselves in a perpetual state of motion, juggling home, work and social responsibilities. Living in this state of constant alert makes it difficult for the mind to shut down when you go to bed; thoughts and plans continue to occupy you and you may sleep fitfully or perhaps not at all. Either way, in the morning, you are not properly rested. What is needed is a program to check that you are fully prepared for a restful night's sleep, and that you are setting yourself up for success in that goal in every way you can.

Assess your situation

Keep a sleep diary for a week to judge your sleep patterns. Fill in a chart with this information in your well-being journal to track success.

DAY	What did I do in the hour before sleep?	What time did I go to bed?	What time did I wake up?	Did I need an alarm to wake?	Did I feel rested upon waking?
Mon					
Tue					
Wed					
Thu					
Fri					
Sat					
Sun					

Prepare your body for sleep

Dr. Chris Idzikowski is the director of the Sleep Assessment and Advisory Service, and the Edinburgh Sleep Center, and is one of the UK's leading experts on sleep and sleep disorders. I've collaborated with him on a project for a UK business and have been fortunate enough to have him share some of his advice for getting a good night's sleep.

1) **Finish your day quietly**

   A good night's sleep only happens in the right environment, so for many people this means setting the scene correctly. Use the hour or two before bed to wind down properly and give an over-stimulated mind and body a chance of a good night's sleep. Avoid things that make your mind race, like e-mails or books and TV programs with an exciting story line. Instead find ways to relax and unwind, such as light reading, a bath, listening to relaxing music or some meditation.

2) **Eat early**

   You will find it difficult to go to sleep if your body is still finishing another task, like digesting food. So don't eat anything three hours before going to bed if possible.

3) **Be wary of stimulants and limit fluid consumption**

   Limit stimulants such as sugar, chocolate, caffeine, alcohol or nicotine as these will stop your body shutting down for sleep. Did you know that it takes around six–eight hours for caffeine to be neutralized in the body? Avoid it from about 2:00 p.m. to make sure it doesn't affect your sleep patterns. Instead switch to fruit tea, decaffeinated versions of your regular drinks (which still do contain some caffeine) or just plain water. And remember that a full bladder will wake you up during the night, so stop drinking about an hour before you go to sleep to give your system time to expel any liquid.

CASE STUDY:
Steven Hyde—how I ran my way to a better night's sleep

I've been lucky to have worked in some very rewarding, though challenging, sales and marketing roles throughout my career. At times the intensity and sheer number of hours required to keep on top of the job have been extremely demanding and 80-hour weeks have not been uncommon. The harder I worked, however, the more difficult I found it to unwind, and this impacted in particular on my sleep. I would often go to bed late after a really tough day's work but still find it hard to drift off. Something else that was sacrificed was exercise—I have always been a keen runner; however, I just didn't have time for it anymore. For the first time in my life I started to feel like I was running out of energy. Then one day, at the end of a particularly stressful day, I got stuck because of an Underground strike that left me stranded in the office at 8:00 p.m.— almost 7 miles from home. If I walked it would take me two and a half hours. However, there was a shopping center right below the office, so I bought some running shoes and shorts, got changed and ran home. It took about an hour, and by the time I got home I felt less stressed and my head was clear. That night I went to bed at a reasonable time and I slept like a baby. I woke the following day feeling refreshed and reenergized. I decided to try this as a new strategy for a month. As a result of my daily run, my energy levels were high, I was sleeping well and was even more focused and driven at work.

4) Avoid vigorous exercise

Exercise is very beneficial in stress management. It aids many bodily functions such as improving circulation and digestion, helps combat stress hormones such as cortisol and adrenaline, and of course, it tires you out, which helps you sleep better. However, exercising too close to bedtime is counterproductive, causing the heart to pump harder and faster and raising the body's core temperature. It would be hard to drift toward restful sleep in such a state. So steer clear of physical exercise in the hour before bed. The exception to this is sexual intercourse, which can lead to deep relaxation and sleep, particularly for men. This is due to a combination of the physical workout plus the cocktail of hormones released during intercourse and orgasm.

Look after your inner child

A good night's sleep is the secret to well-behaved children, according to a recent study by Finnish researchers. They observed that sleep-deprived children may not appear tired, but the less sleep they have, the more hyperactive they become. In the survey the best-behaved children were those who regularly got more than eight hours' sleep every night. What would you do to prepare a child for bed? If you don't have children you may not be sure quite how to answer that, but once upon a time you used to be a child, so think of how your parents prepared you for bed. What kinds of things would you do to relax children in preparation for sleep? Perhaps run them a warm bath, give them a cup of warm milk, read them a bedtime story, sing them a lullaby, give them a cuddle or possibly a massage. Think about what you would avoid doing. Once a child is asleep, parents often go to the living room, turn on the television, make themselves a cup of coffee or pour themselves a glass of wine, fire up the laptop or start fiddling with their BlackBerry or iPhone. Even though we know it is important to have a wind-down or relaxation routine to prepare a child for bed, many of us do not look after ourselves with the same care and attention that we would a child. Surely we deserve the same.

Aim to nurture yourself as you would a child before you go to sleep: disengage your brain and relax physically with some of these suggestions:

- **Turn off the TV** and have a relaxing conversation with someone instead.
- **Take a warm bath** complete with aromatherapy oils (lavender is a good one for aiding sleep, or try neroli or sandalwood); four or five drops will be enough.
- **Try meditation** by lighting a candle and focusing on the flame for an effective technique that allows you to ignore other distractions.
- **Play relaxing music**.
- **Practice your breathing exercises** (see Chapter 7).
- **Make a connection with someone.** If you live with a partner, pay that person some attention. Tell someone you love them or call a friend to say hello. At the very least try hugging someone; this helps raise your endorphin level—the body's natural "high"— which helps you relax.
- **Massage someone else's neck**, it's an excellent way to wind down. You will get much appreciation for the massage, and the person is sure to return the favor. Alternatively, try stroking your cat or dog (an activity shown to reduce blood pressure). Or massage your own neck and shoulders.

Create your ideal sleep haven

The human brain is a very powerful resource and it largely works by association. Give it the right cues and it can immediately take you to related places and memories. A particular song might take you back to a specific time in your life, or a perfume will remind you of a specific person. The brain is so powerful that it can achieve this effect sometimes years after the original association was made. Use this knowledge to your advantage by helping your brain immediately recognize your bedroom as a place where you rest, so that when you walk through the door your body starts to relax and prepare for sleep. There are really just two things you should be doing in that room: sleeping; and being intimate with your partner. Your goal is to make the bedroom a haven that you associate with just those two activities.

Analyze what you currently use your bedroom for. Is it for sleep? Or do you also work in there, read, eat, smoke, watch TV in bed or do the ironing? Is it tidy and organized so that it doesn't distract from going to sleep? Or is it messy, cluttered with books and clothes? Some people even work on their laptops from bed—do you want to associate your grumpy old boss with your bedroom?

Deal with dust mites

Some basic equipment in the quest for a good night's sleep are your bed and bedding. And for the ultimate stress-free night's sleep, you should take good care of them to reduce the spread of dust mites. The average bed is home to hundreds of thousands of these microscopic organisms and 10 percent of the weight of a two-year-old pillow can be composed of dead mites and their droppings. They eat dead human and animal skin cells and produce waste droppings at an alarming rate. These droppings contain a protein which can cause an allergic reaction in humans; symptoms range from itchy eyes to asthma attacks and can affect anyone of any age. So to ensure you eliminate this potential stress to your health, tackle dust mites in the following ways:

- Buy a mite-resistant cover for your mattress, duvet and pillows.
- Change your sheets regularly and vacuum your mattress before turning it.

- Vacuum your bedroom carpets, or remove them and have wooden floors instead, which don't harbor the mites.
- Wash bed linen at the highest temperature possible.
- Keep the room temperature below 68°F (see page 69 on why this helps you to sleep better).
- Keep soft toys off children's beds and either wash them regularly at a high temperature or place them in the freezer to kill the bugs.

Evict the electrics

When creating an ideal haven for sleep, be careful about what you let into your bedroom in the first place. Your body has an electric stimulus that keeps your heart beating, your brain working and even gives you a jolt when you touch silver paper or a metal filling in your mouth. However, your body's natural electrical flow can be interfered with by the electromagnetic frequencies given off by devices and gadgets in your bedroom, and this could prevent you from ever achieving a really deep and satisfying sleep. Even if they are turned off (i.e., not on standby), electronic devices will still have electricity flowing through them. Therefore consider ridding your bedroom of as many as possible to maximize your good night's sleep. Make it a resolution that from now on you will use your bedroom only for the two purposes it was intended and ensure that everything else happens in another room.

Use your senses

By engaging your senses you can relax your body using some of these techniques:

- **Smell**: naturally perfumed linen spray on your pillow or sheets will help you fall asleep; lavender, neroli and sandalwood all have great sleep-inducing benefits.

- **Sound**: neutralize the effects of a noisy environment with white noise (noise containing many frequencies). This gives you something to focus on and helps you detach from the original distraction. Zone out everything from dogs barking to cars passing by tuning your radio to static and listening to that. Or buy a CD of the sound of the ocean or birdsong and play that instead.

CASE STUDY:
Aegon Welsh, celebrity personal trainer and ex-special forces

When I left the armed forces and started my personal fitness company, my schedule meant that I didn't get enough sleep over a prolonged period. I was aware that I was starting to make silly errors—forgetting things, making poor decisions, that sort of thing. I even turned up a day early for a flight to Los Angeles! It seemed like my mental capacity was deteriorating and I had a permanent fuzzy head. As soon as I'd set up the company and started working with clients, my schedule got back into balance. As I got more sleep, I noticed that my memory and mental capability improved. My mood was better, decisions came easier and I stopped being forgetful. I'd estimate that I got another 15 percent out of each working day just because I turned up to work well rested. Now I work with many personalities devising personal fitness programs and exercise plans. As part of the routine, I always do a lifestyle audit and check out their sleep pattern. If it's not right, we change it. You can't have a toned body if you have a fuzzy head!

- **Sight**: rest in a dark room. Melatonin is a hormone that helps your body clock to function properly, instructing the body when to sleep and for how long, but it is triggered only when it gets dark. If you spend your day and night in bright conditions, then melatonin production can stop altogether. So turn off the lights and put up blackout curtains or blinds that completely block the light from outside.

- **Temperature**: many people sleep in rooms that are too warm or too cool. During sleep our core body temperature drops and we become more sensitive to room temperature and trying to adjust to variations during the night; for example, when the heating goes off. This is a disturbance that keeps us in light rather than deep sleep. Try turning the bedroom heating down and aim for a cool room (64°F) and a warm duvet instead.

Start your day the gentle way

If you get enough sleep, you will awaken naturally at the right time without the help of an alarm clock. If you do want the backup of an alarm, however, look for one that wakes you naturally in the morning; for example, with a gradual increase of light or natural sounds like birdsongs. This is a much kinder start to the day than a traditional alarm that jolts you awake and panics your system into producing the fight-or-flight hormones adrenaline and cortisol.

When you're awake, open the curtains to let in the daylight. This will help your natural body clock stop producing the sleep-inducing melatonin and understand that it is time to wake up.

Spend a few minutes preparing your mind for the day, either meditating or just focusing on what you have planned. Then get active to get the blood coursing through your veins and stimulate your circulation. Tune the radio to a music station and dance along to what you hear, go for a short run, do some stretches or some yoga. Finally, drink a glass of hot water with a slice of lemon in it to help to flush toxins from your system, and refuel for the day with a healthy breakfast of oats, fruit and nuts to keep you going all morning.

MY PERSONAL ACTION PLAN

I promise myself I am going to improve my sleep patterns by taking these actions:

1. _____

2. _____

3. _____

4. _____

5. _____

Enter your commitments in your well-being journal to log your actions and progress.

CHAPTER 7

STEP 3:

Practice deep breathing

What are the three most important things that we need to do to stay alive? Breathe, drink water and eat food. These will be the focus for the next three chapters, starting with breathing. You can go several weeks (if not months) without eating, you can go several days without water; however, we can only go a few minutes (at most) without oxygen.

ASSESS YOUR BREATHING

Do you ever suffer from breathlessness or shortness of breath?	Y/N
Do you find you usually take short, shallow rapid breaths?	Y/N
Do you ever suffer from a fuzzy mind or brain fog?	Y/N
Do you feel out of breath climbing the stairs?	Y/N
Does it feel difficult or uncomfortable to take a full, deep breath from your belly?	Y/N
When under stress do you find that:	
it's difficult to concentrate?	Y/N
you make poor decisions?	Y/N
you become clumsy?	Y/N

If you answered yes to all or most of those questions, you need some help. Stress is having an impact on your breathing, and this chapter will give you a great start, with many practical suggestions on improving your breathing to ensure your body is always well oxygenated, in turn better equipping you to deal with the daily stresses we face. Even if you do not have concerns about stress impacting your breathing, the techniques below can be used to remain calm and relaxed in times of stress and anxiety.

A LIFE SOURCE

Oxygen is the most important nutrient of the body—every cell needs it to function efficiently; however, the brain is the body's largest user of oxygen. Even though it makes up less than 5 percent of the body's total weight, the brain consumes the most amount of the body's oxygen—about 20 percent. In old age, when arteries become clogged, and the supply of blood and oxygen to the brain is reduced, people can become senile, irritable and dull.

Breathing serves two purposes: it helps in ingesting oxygen to be transported to all parts of the body through the bloodstream, and it helps in the elimination of waste products. The oxygen purifies the blood and helps in burning the waste products. It provides energy to all parts of the body. When the flow of oxygen to the brain is completely cut off, a person will lose consciousness within 10 seconds. Brain cells are destroyed after four to six minutes without oxygen so extended periods without it flowing to the brain leads to brain damage and ultimately death. The rate at which we inhale and exhale is controlled by the respiratory center within the medulla oblongata in the brain. Interestingly this is also the part of the brain that instigates the stress response.

More oxygen will clear your mind, rejuvenate your skin and energize your whole body. On the other hand, lack of oxygen will lead to mental sluggishness, lack of focus, depression and anxiety.

CASE STUDY:
Neil Shah, mountaineer

I discovered the hazards of a lack of oxygen when I spent some time in the Himalayas climbing Mount Everest. When you get to altitudes of 8,200 feet and above the air begins to thin, which makes it harder for us to function. The higher we go the more challenging it becomes so that by the time you get to 16,400 or 19,600 feet your pace slows to a crawl and even tying your shoelaces can leave you exhausted and gasping for air. You can't think clearly, you feel dizzy and light-headed, your head is pounding, you may slur your words, your brain–body connection begins to fail and you literally feel punch-drunk. The lack of oxygen is impacting on your body's most basic functions. As you continue ascending you will eventually get to a point where the amount of oxygen is not enough to sustain human life. This point is generally above 26,200 feet and is known as the death zone. Many deaths in high-altitude mountaineering have been caused by the effects of the death zone, either directly due to a loss of vital functions or indirectly as a result of poor decisions made under stress or a physical weakening leading to an accident. Once you are in the death zone, no human body can acclimatize to the altitude. An extended stay in the zone without supplementary oxygen will result in deterioration of bodily functions, loss of consciousness and, ultimately, death.

HOW DO WE BREATHE?

1) **You inhale**

When you inhale, as you take a breath in, oxygen enters the body through the nose and passes into the windpipe or trachea. The trachea splits into two tubes called the bronchi, which in turn connect to the lungs. These bronchi then branch into smaller bronchioles. A muscle beneath the ribs called the diaphragm then contracts, which reduces pressure in the chest cavity and creates suction. This causes the lungs to expand and take in air. The diaphragm then flattens and moves downward and the rib cage then swings up and out. By increasing in size, this decreases the internal air pressure, and so air from outside the body (which is now at a higher pressure than inside the chest thorax) rushes into the lungs to equalize the pressure.

2) **Oxygen moves through the lungs**

Once oxygen is inside the lungs, it travels from the bronchioles to millions of tiny capsules, or sacs, called alveoli. Within these alveoli, oxygen is exchanged for carbon dioxide. The fresh oxygen is transported throughout the body by red blood cells in the arteries. The tissues in the body use oxygen for energy.

3) **Carbon dioxide is expelled**

While utilizing oxygen, the body's cells produce carbon dioxide, which is a by-product that the body cannot use. The bloodstream moves the carbon dioxide through the veins back to the lungs. Upon exhalation, the diaphragm and intercostal muscles (the muscles between the ribs) relax and return to their resting positions. This reduces the size of the thoracic cavity, thereby increasing the pressure and forcing the carbon dioxide out of the lungs, up through the trachea and out of the nose and mouth.

BREATHE DEEPLY

The benefits of breathing correctly include purifying the blood, creating an upsurge in energy, and relaxing your body and mind. Bad breathing habits lead to an imbalance of oxygen and carbon dioxide in the body. If you are looking for relief from stress, practicing deep breathing is one of the best services that you could be doing for yourself. Even under normal circumstances, taking a full, deep breath by itself is deeply relaxing. However, most of us are used to "shallow breathing": using only 25–30 percent of our lung capacity.

TEST YOUR BREATH

Check to see if your breath is slow or fast. Count the number of inhalations you take over one minute; this will give you your respiration rate. Are you taking more than 30 breaths per minute? If so, your breathing is shallow and fast, which suggests you are stressed.

Now take a few slow, deep breaths. Be aware of what parts of your body are moving. Is the breath being driven from the chest or the belly? Are the shoulders moving? What else are you aware of? Do you have any difficulty breathing? Short, shallow breaths leave you panicked, anxious, confused and lacking focus. Practice slow, deep belly breaths to maintain a relaxed state.

Unless you live atop a mountain, the chances are you live in an environment that has a plentiful supply of oxygen, it is freely available and is still free of cost, so why is it many of us have an oxygen deficit? Have you ever paid attention to your breathing? When you tested your breath did you find it was shallow and rapid? This is one of the harmful effects of stress and tension. Our modern-day lifestyle is exposing us to various tensions and stresses and one of the casualties of this is the quality of our breathing. A shallow breath fails to bring sufficient oxygen to the body, and also fails to cleanse the body of all the waste products, which can ultimately weaken the body's capacity to fight disease and result in sleep disorders, anxiety, stomach upset, heartburn and dizziness.

LEARN TO BREATHE CORRECTLY

Correct breathing has long been a central tenet of many Eastern religions. The practice of "*pranayama*" or "extension of the life force" is central to yoga where the breath is known as "*prana*" or "life force." Perfect balance is achieved by learning to breathe properly. Just the practice of learning how to breathe properly will take you a long way toward better mental and physical health as well as help you in managing your stress levels.

An ideal way to relieve stress is through breathing exercises. These exercises are incredibly effective and can be performed pretty much anywhere and at almost any time! They don't take long to perform, are very easy to do—and are free.

Let me teach you a few basic breathing techniques to help you relax and reenergize. Please do not simply accept my word for the benefits of any of the following exercises; I encourage you to approach these techniques as scientists. Before you start each technique assess how you feel: look around the room at colors, contours and shapes; notice what sounds you're aware of and even your posture. Then be aware of any changes when you finish each exercise. If you notice any positive benefits, you may have found a useful technique in equipping you to combat stress. If you feel no benefit you never need to do the exercises. So have an open mind, give them a go and see what happens.

Exercise 1: Natural breath

Let's start with your basic natural breath. When you assessed your breathing earlier did you find you were breathing using your chest or using your belly? When a baby takes a breath you will notice that its belly will inflate with every inhalation and deflate with every exhalation. If you are breathing from your chest the rib cage restricts inflation of the lungs, so breathing more deeply using your belly allows you to use 100 percent of your lung capacity. So why do so many of us not breathe like babies anymore?

When I demonstrate this exercise in seminars and workshops, a lot of people look at me and say they don't feel comfortable breathing from their belly because it makes them look fat. It is important to bear in mind that if you are conscious of how it looks when you take a deep, true breath and you use it as a reason not to breathe correctly, then for reasons of vanity you are depriving yourself of valuable oxygen! But vanity is not the only reason that we do not breathe in the way that we did as children.

What happens to a muscle that you don't use very often? It suffers from atrophy—it literally wastes away. What about a muscle that you exercise daily? It becomes stronger, more defined, possibly more flexible. There are various muscles involved with the breathing process, such as the diaphragm and the intercostal muscles. If they are not used correctly or effectively, they too can become weaker or less efficient. This in turn can make it harder (or even feel unnatural) to take a full deep belly breath.

I would like to remind you to breathe in the way that you did as a baby. And if you would like a practical demonstration of this exercise, just find a baby and copy what they are doing! Do bear in mind that when babies are born they are not taught how to breathe. They just do what comes naturally. I would like you to be aware of your natural, baby breath.

1) Sit or stand with your feet firmly flat on the floor.
2) Now imagine a triangle that begins at your belly button; the other two corners of the triangle are on your hips. Inside that triangle there is a ball or a balloon.
3) When you take a breath in, visualize the breath slowly inflating the ball or the balloon. At the top of the breath hold for a few seconds and then slowly release, deflating the ball or balloon and pulling your navel to your spine.
4) Repeat this for a few minutes and notice what changes you are aware of.

Are you feeling even slightly more calm or relaxed? Look around the room—has the brightness or sharpness of the lights changed in any way? Do things look brighter or sharper? What about sounds—are you more aware of any background noises or are other noises louder? You may be aware of some subtle changes simply from breathing as nature intended you to, but at the very least you should feel more calm and relaxed. Practice this regularly and in particular when you are stressed. The more time that you spend breathing deeply the easier it becomes. Soon enough you will be breathing just like you did when you were a baby and gaining all the health and well-being associated with a natural deep breath.

Exercise 2: Breathing for stress relief

The following technique can also be done anywhere and at virtually any time; it is a simple technique with profound benefits. These factors make this stress-relief breathing exercise one of my most popular and convenient tension tamers. Here's how the basic controlled breathing technique works:

1) Stand or sit in a comfortable, relaxed position with your spine erect.
2) Inhale slowly through your nose to the count of 5. Imagine a ball or balloon in your belly inflating.
3) Hold the breath in the ball or balloon in your belly for 5–10 seconds.
4) Count slowly to 8 as you exhale.
5) Repeat this technique several times.

Tips

- As you breathe, let your abdomen expand outward, rather than raising your shoulders (see Exercise 1 on pages 77–78). This is a more relaxed and natural way to breathe, and helps your lungs fill themselves more fully with fresh air, releasing more "old" air. You can do this just a few times to release tension, or for several minutes as a form of meditation.
- If you like, you can make your throat a little tighter as you exhale so the air comes out like a whisper. This type of breathing is used in some forms of yoga and can add additional tension relief.
- You may find it useful to light a candle and focus on the flame to give you a visual distraction.

Exercise 3: Alternate nostril breathing

Are you a left nostril or a right nostril breather? This ancient brain-balancing breathing technique is designed to produce optimum functioning in both sides of the brain. Your brain has two hemispheres that control different functions: the left brain controls the right-hand side of the body and is often thought of as the logical, thinking side. It controls functions such as speech, reasoning, writing and numerical skills. The right brain controls the left-hand side of the body. It is often thought of as the creative, imaginative side. Activities associated with the right brain include art, sports, music, exploration and dreaming.

We do not breathe evenly in both nostrils—at one time one nostril is working harder than the other. If you hold a finger under your nostrils and exhale hard you will notice which one is working harder for you at the moment. You will find it is easier to breathe through one than the other. Each nostril alternates about every two to three hours.

Scientists have discovered that the nasal cycle corresponds with brain function. The electrical activity of the brain was found to be greater on the side opposite the less congested nostril. The research showed that when a person's left nostril was less obstructed, the right side of the brain was predominant. Test subjects were indeed found to do better on creative tests. Similarly when the right nostril was less obstructed the left side of the brain was predominant. Test subjects did better on verbal skills.

Alternate nostril breathing balances the amount of oxygenated blood that each side of the brain will receive and in turn leads to a balance between our creative and logical thinking ability. It is also a very effective technique to calm the mind and bring balance to the nervous system. Imagine you are working on your accounts and your creative mind is working more efficiently—not only are you not in the best state to be working with numbers, you may also end up adopting a creative attitude in solving your accounting problem!

The technique below clears any blockage to the airflow in the nostrils and reestablishes the natural nasal cycle.

1) Place a finger under your nostrils and exhale through your nose. One nostril will be working harder than the other. This changes according to activity and it swaps throughout the day.
2) Close your right nostril using the back of your left thumb.
3) Inhale from your left nostril to the count of four.

4) Let go of the right nostril and gently pinch the left nostril with your left ring finger and hold for the count of 16.

5) Exhale through your right nostril for eight counts.

6) Repeat on the other side, swapping fingers.

Exercise 4: Mindful breathing

Jon Kabat-Zinn (a renowned teacher of mindfulness meditation and the founder of the Mindfulness-Based Stress Reduction program at the University of Massachusetts Medical Center) describes mindfulness as: "paying attention in a particular way; on purpose, in the present moment, and nonjudgmentally."

Mindfulness is the art of consciously directing our awareness. "Mindfulness" and "awareness" are terms that are often used interchangeably; however, that can lead to confusion. For example, you may be aware that you are irritable; however, that doesn't mean that you are being mindful of your irritability. In order to be mindful you have to be consciously aware of yourself, not just vaguely aware. Knowing that you are eating a banana is different from eating a banana mindfully.

So let's look again at eating, as it's a good example of how mindfulness works. Often, when we eat, we are doing other things as well. We are eating a sandwich in front of the computer as we work, we are sitting in front of the TV watching our favorite shows with our dinner in our lap, we are talking or reading, we are doing many of these things at the same time. And what happens then is that we are so focused on other things that we are less conscious of tastes and textures, the smells and flavors of our food. Have you ever finished eating but you can't remember what you ate? You probably weren't conscious of your thoughts wandering away from your food, so there was no conscious effort to bring your focus back to what was on your plate. In other words, there was no purposefulness to what you were doing, and purposefulness is a very important part of mindfulness.

In contrast, let's look at purposeful eating. You have turned off the television or have decided to take a break away from your desk. You look at the food in front of you and notice how it smells. Each mouthful you take, you are aware of the tastes and textures and you are noticing how you are reacting to these sensations. If your mind happens to wander, you will notice that too, and deliberately bring your focus back to the process of eating. You are eating mindfully, in other words. Allowing yourself to actively experience what you are doing—whether it's the consciousness of your breath in meditation, giving yourself permission to feel emotion rather than suppressing it or during the simple act of eating—means that your mind is being actively shaped by your thoughts.

1) Sit upright, with your spine erect and feet flat on the floor in a comfortable and relaxed position.

2) Be aware of your present state and existence. Block out any unwanted or disruptive thoughts. Closing your eyes will help you focus.

3) Focus on every detail of your breathing. Breathe in slowly through your nose for several seconds. Be aware of the chest and then the belly inflating and filling with air. Bring awareness to how it feels to take a full deep breath. Notice the sensations in your body and the growing feelings of inner comfort and relaxation.

4) Breathe out through your mouth, ensuring that the exhalation lasts twice as long as the inhalation.

5) Maintain your mindful breathing for three to five minutes.

If you like, you can increase the practice to 15–20 minutes per day. With regular practice, you can train your body to relax in stressful situations by using this exercise. This exercise can also be effective in dealing with anxiety, panic attacks, stage fright and fears (such as the

CASE STUDY:
Simone Beech, Events Manager—how I used breathing to overcome panic attacks

After a particularly traumatic experience in my life, I became prone to panic attacks. I would find that stress or uncomfortable, threatening situations would cause me to hyperventilate and as my breathing became shallow and fast I would become more panicky. The fear of a panic attack would increase the feelings of panic. I would feel dizzy and light-headed, have heart palpitations, chest pains and feel my throat tightening. My vision would become blurry, I would have shortness of breath, feel nauseous, have a desperate urge to go to the bathroom and sometimes uncontrollable trembling. On a few occasions it happened at a work event. Yet after being taught a simple breathing technique by a colleague, I found I could stave off a panic attack. I simply looked 22 yards beyond where I was standing and in my mind began noting what I could see. While doing this I would take one deep breath in through my nose for four seconds. I was told to fill my lungs with air. Then I would hold my breath for five seconds. Finally I would release my breath through my mouth for five seconds. I would then turn 90 degrees to the right and repeat this exercise. After I had gone through this exercise four times, I would have come full circle and would be back to where I had started from. Taking a few minutes to move the focus from my rising feelings of panic to what I was aware of outside of myself and to regulate my breathing was enough to prevent the panic attack from taking place.

fear of flying). Taking a restorative pause to focus on your breathing can also be a valuable anger-management tool. Find a quiet corner or a cubicle, or even practice in the bathroom.

Exercise 5: Energizing breathing

This exercise is called "bellows breath" as it mimics the workings of a bellows that is used to fan a fire. This is a natural alternative to a stimulant such as coffee and is an exercise that I use regularly. I use it to pump myself up before getting on stage to run a seminar, or before playing soccer on a Thursday evening. It pumps air and life force vigorously and dynamically throughout the entire system. When practicing this exercise, be ready for an energizing workout as it is the ultimate exercise for energy and power!

1) Sit up in a comfortable position with your feet flat on the floor.
2) Stretch your spine upward, lengthen your neck and subtly bring your chin back and in, like a soldier at attention. This will align your spine with the back of your head.
3) Close your eyes.
4) Relax your stomach muscles.
5) Now begin to breathe as forcefully as comfortable through the nose with equal emphasis on the inhalation and exhalation. The diaphragm should expand and contract in conjunction with your breathing. All the breaths should be deep and powerful and you should establish a steady rhythm. The pace should be about one second for inhalation and about the same for exhalation.
6) Do a round of 10 repetitions and then inhale completely, hold your breath in for 1–5 seconds and then exhale completely. This completes one round.
7) Take a short break.
8) Slowly work your way up to doing five rounds.

Next we can bring hand movement into it if you are in an environment where this is possible.

1) Inhale and raise your arms up above your head (your biceps should be next to your ears).
2) Exhale vigorously and pull your arms down and your elbows into the ribs at the same time.
3) You can then repeat this in three sets of 30, first slow, then medium and finally very fast.

As you complete these exercises you should feel warmer, more awake, more alert, more energized and naturally more confident and relaxed.

What changes are you aware of?

Did you stop to assess the changes you noticed after each exercise? Whatever changes that you are aware of, you achieved them yourself, without any pills and potions, without spending any money, without employing any special equipment, and there are no side effects to these exercises! You had everything you need on board already. Just by using your breath you were easily, effectively and efficiently able to change your state and how you were feeling!

MY PERSONAL ACTION PLAN

I promise myself I am going to improve my breathing by taking these actions:

1. _____

2. _____

3. _____

4. _____

5. _____

Enter your commitments in your well-being journal to log your actions and progress.

CHAPTER 8

STEP 4:

Stay hydrated

Water is the most important nutrient for our bodies after oxygen. We could survive only a few days without drinking water and it's impossible to go through your day-to-day life without being aware of water's importance. We see that message everywhere—from the covers of magazines proclaiming that water will give you flawless skin to newspaper articles and features on TV. And it's true: water is vital for the processes in our bodies to function properly and our skin looks better when it's properly hydrated, and proper hydration varies from person to person and on activity levels—whether that amount is 6 cups per day, 8 cups or even 7 pints.

But perhaps less well known is the effect water—or the lack of it—has on our brains.

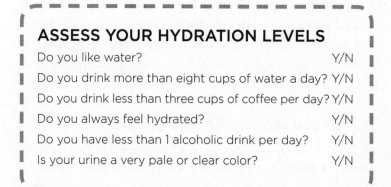

ASSESS YOUR HYDRATION LEVELS

Do you like water?   Y/N

Do you drink more than eight cups of water a day? Y/N

Do you drink less than three cups of coffee per day? Y/N

Do you always feel hydrated?   Y/N

Do you have less than 1 alcoholic drink per day?   Y/N

Is your urine a very pale or clear color?   Y/N

If you answered no to all or most of those questions, you need some help. This chapter will give you a great start, with many practical suggestions on improving your hydration and understanding why this is important when combating stress.

WHY IS WATER SO IMPORTANT?

The human body is approximately 70 percent water. The effect that water has on our brains is probably best understood when we understand that our brains are made up of approximately 85 percent water. Clearly then, when we are not hydrated properly enough, we can experience anything from mild headaches and fatigue to seizures, which can be a symptom of severe hydration. As you've probably experienced, when you haven't drunk enough water, your energy levels are lower and the more tired you feel.

And the more tired you feel, the more prone you are to stress. There is, in fact, a chemical reason why you get more stressed, as when you're even mildly dehydrated cortisol levels in the body increase, and as we have seen (see page 17), cortisol production is triggered by the stress response. And one way to balance these chemicals in your brain? Drink more water.

So if you're looking for a simple way to unwind from your stress-filled life, try drinking a glass of water—it will help you to cope better with stressful situations. If you're not a water drinker, carry a bottle around with you (preferably glass as it doesn't contaminate the water with any chemicals in the way plastic might) and try taking a few sips every 15 minutes. If you drink a lot of soda try swapping it for sparkling water.

How do you know if you're dehydrated?

Do you feel thirsty? That means you are already dehydrated. Another way to check is by looking at your pee after you go to the bathroom.

Light-colored and odorless? You are well hydrated. Dark-colored and smelly? You are dehydrated, and the more dehydrated you are, the darker and smellier your pee becomes.

How much water should you drink each day?

It has been estimated that daily our bodies lose about 10 cups of water just through functioning normally. This water must be replaced every day from the water we drink and the food we eat, but how much water you should drink depends on several things: the size of your body, how physically active you are, and even the climate—because your body works hard to keep you warm or cool. As a general guideline, the average person should drink between 2.5 and 6 pints every day to replace the bodily fluids normally lost throughout the day. If you're living in a hot climate and exercising a lot, you'd be at the higher end of that range; if you're in a cooler climate and mostly sedentary, you'd need less.

WHO (World Health Organization) recommendations for daily water requirements

	Average conditions	Manual labor in high temperatures	Total needs in pregnancy/lactation
Female adults	4 pints	8 pints	Pregnancy: 8.5 pints Lactation: 9.5 pints
Male adults	5 pints	8 pints	

SIPPING STRESS AWAY

Does this sound too simple? There is a clear link between water and stress reduction. To function properly, all of our body's processes and organs need to be well hydrated. When you are dehydrated, your body cannot perform at its optimum capacity and that can lead to stress. Research has shown that even mild dehydration can increase cortisol levels, whereas staying well hydrated can keep your stress levels down. When you don't give your body the fluids it needs, you're putting stress on it, and it's going to react negatively. Suffice to say drinking lots of water and staying well hydrated will not cause your money problems to magically disappear, nor your deadlines at work or the traffic jam on your commute, but it will not exacerbate any of these stressors with the added burden of the stress your body feels through being dehydrated.

Break the cycle of stress and dehydration

We have now established that stress can cause dehydration and vice versa. The symptoms of stress and dehydration are very similar—increased heart rate, nausea, fatigue and headaches. Do also bear in mind that when suffering from stress you are far more likely to get dehydrated as your heart rate is up and you are breathing more heavily, causing you to lose fluid. In addition, during times of stress you are much more likely to forget to drink and eat well. You get yourself stuck in a vicious cycle; however, it's good to know that breaking the cycle is easy: just ensure you drink more water throughout the day.

Here are some of my top suggestions for ensuring you get the water that you need:

- Invest in a means of filtering your water—these range from free-standing pitchers with filter cartridges to more sophisticated purification systems.
- Measure out the day's water in the morning and fill two 1¾-pint bottles (or the quantity your body needs; see table on page 89) with your filtered water and take it to work. This makes drinking

good-quality water more convenient and also helps you keep track of how much water is being drunk that day.

- Drink small amounts of water *throughout* the day. Eight glasses all at once isn't good for you as most of it will pass straight through your system, have you dashing for the bathroom, and you won't see the benefits.

- Add a squirt of fresh lemon or lime juice to your glass of water to vary the taste. You can also use a few sprigs of crushed fresh mint or another herb for variety. I often add a little cinnamon powder.

- Try drinking a caffeine-free herbal tea. Currently my favorite herbal tea is rooibos. It tastes as refreshing as regular tea but it has no caffeine. Remember that even though green tea has health benefits, it also has caffeine.

- Keep a glass of water next to your bed; many of us wake up dehydrated first thing in the morning.

If there are certain places and times in your life when you know you're under extra stress—at work, on your daily commute, during exercise—be sure to have a bottle of water with you to sip during those high-stress times.

Ditch the fizz

Stop drinking all sodas, caffeinated drinks and juices for a week and replace them with water and see how you feel. If you are a caffeine addict (as I was), you may suffer from cold turkey if you withdraw completely (symptoms can include headaches); however, the more water you drink, the easier it will be to manage. Hang in there! Notice the impact it has on your energy, your well-being, your focus and concentration, your sleep and your skin. Document your progress in your well-being journal.

CASE STUDY:
Neil Shah, how replacing soda with water changed my life

Most people that know me know that I have a passionate dislike of sodas. I would never drink such products and would actively try to dissuade someone from drinking them in my presence (my colleague Anisha has taken to hiding her occasional bottle of cola in her office drawer in fear of being lectured!).

What most people may not know is that I used to drink sodas all the time as a child and teenager. In fact I pretty much lived off cola and avoided water where possible. At school I could easily get through four cans of soda a day. Then when I got to college I got "wise" and started thinking about my health, so I turned to diet versions. They're filled with nasty chemicals like phosphoric acid that can literally rot your teeth and stomach lining. The artificial sweeteners (such as aspartame) in these drinks react with the hydrochloric acid in your stomach to create formaldehyde. This highly toxic chemical is used to embalm dead bodies. It's frightening to think that many people are slowly embalming themselves while still alive!

On a trip to Africa in my late twenties I visited a drought zone and was shocked at how a lack of water can devastate life. It really helped me to put things in perspective. Speaking to a charity worker in a refugee camp, I was shocked to learn that most Americans and Europeans are also chronically dehydrated. And they have permanent access to running water! I returned to London committed to change. I began drinking virtually nothing but water. I eliminated all carbonated drinks from my dietary intake, as well as most juice and other noncarbonated drinks. I felt much healthier, had better energy and the acne that had plagued me for years began to clear up.

MY PERSONAL ACTION PLAN

I promise myself I am going to improve my water intake and hydration levels by taking these actions:

1. _____

2. _____

3. _____

4. _____

5. _____

Enter your commitments in your well-being journal to log your actions and progress.

CHAPTER 9

STEP 5:

Eat for well-being NOT for stress

Like oxygen and water, food is vital for our health and well-being—it is our energy source and provides our bodies with the nutrients it needs to grow, fight disease and repair itself. Food can affect our stress levels in two ways: it can either be the cause of the stress—the physical stress caused to the body and its organs as it gamely tries to assimilate and metabolize what we eat and drink; or it can simply aggravate or increase the stress from which we are already suffering. Many of us feed ourselves platefuls of food loaded with toxins, chemicals, fats, sugars and other nasties that are of no benefit to our bodies and we expect it to cope. And, even if we eat relatively well, the pace of modern life is such that many of us gulp down half-chewed mouthfuls while sitting in front of our computers or staring at a television screen, thus putting strains on our digestive systems. So let us start by assessing if our diet is causing us stress or promoting well-being.

If you answer no to all or most of the following questions, you need some help. This chapter will give you a great start, with many practical suggestions on improving your diet to ensure that it is not causing or increasing stress.

ASSESS YOUR DIET

Do you have a healthy balanced diet?   Y/N

Do you eat regular meals (at least three a day)?   Y/N

Do you eat breakfast (within an hour of waking up)?   Y/N

Do you eat five portions of vegetables per day?   Y/N

Do you eat red meat less than twice per week?   Y/N

Do you eat takeout food less than once per week?   Y/N

Do you eat fresh, home-prepared meals more than prepared frozen dinners?   Y/N

Are the majority of your meals prepared without a microwave?   Y/N

FOOD AND STRESS

There has always been a link between stress and nutrition. When your stress is at a constantly high level, your body can be depleted of vital nutrients leaving you vulnerable to the negative effects of stress, which include a weakened immune response, heart disease and high blood pressure. But you can help tackle damagingly high stress levels by practicing proper self-care techniques and following a healthy diet.

A balanced diet will boost our resistance against the effects that stress brings upon the body, therefore it is important to constantly fill up on vital nutrients. Someone with a healthy and balanced diet is likely to be far less stressed than someone with a poor diet, as the healthy body is working more efficiently and is more resilient to stress.

Poor eating habits

One of the main issues with stress is that it can cause unhealthy eating habits. This applies mainly to people who are always on the go and lead a busy lifestyle. They often endure large amounts of stress and have no time to fit a balanced diet around their busy schedule. Additionally, as we have seen in Chapter 4, stress makes the body crave foods that are high in fats and sugars. This flaw in eating will, in time, inflict a greater stress on the body, plus other problems that pose a threat to your physical and mental health. Conversely, having a good balance of the vitamins and minerals in your body can aid in reducing stress, as we will see.

Imbalances in the blood sugar

When someone stressed does not eat the right amount of food or the correct amount of nutrients, they will start to encounter inconsistencies in their blood sugars. These inconsistencies lead to the person not behaving as they normally would. They may experience:

- Tiredness
- Lapses of concentration
- Mood swings

If stress is not dealt with properly in the short term, in the long term the body may suffer from more serious blood sugar problems, such as diabetes.

Breakfast—is yours setting you up for the day?

First thing in the morning your alarm goes off (causing stress) and you drag yourself from a restful state. You reach for your first cup of caffeine and probably a food high in refined sugars such as a slice of toast with jam or a sugar-loaded cereal. But by the time you reach work, those refined sugars may have shut down your essential systems. The body can work efficiently with only about three teaspoons of sugar in the bloodstream at any given time, yet the average bowl of sugary cereal can contain up to 12 teaspoons of sugar. Over three teaspoons and your body's systems may be suppressed for up to six hours as your body desperately uses its principal resources to fight to process all that sugar and normalize its blood sugar levels. The result—your body is in a state of stress. So, rather than reaching for the refined sugary cereal, opt for breakfast options such as eggs or oats, which contain protein and sustained slow-release carbohydrates, providing you with useable energy (see pages 100–103) and beneficial nutrients. Surprisingly, even a cooked breakfast will fuel you better because it doesn't contain all that sugar and still contains proteins and more useful energy—just opt for grilled, not fried versions of your breakfast favorites to keep the fat content down.

Forgetting or skipping meals

Most people know that it is important to eat three meals a day, but stress can have the effect of making people skip or forget to eat their meals. They find that later in the day they will become hungry, and more than likely resort to eating junk or fast food to resolve their hunger quickly. To help balance your energy levels and keep them regular, design a meal plan for the day that incorporates a big meal in the morning, something relatively light for lunch and another light meal in the evening. In between meals reach for healthy snacks if you are hungry, such as nuts, seeds, fruit, nut butters or vegetable sticks with low-fat dip. Eating regularly will prevent fluctuations in your blood sugar levels. Prepare your meals in advance—I prepare my breakfast and lunch the night before, so no matter how busy I get at work I know that the right foods are waiting for me.

Before you go for your weekly grocery shopping create a meal plan for the week ahead. This will ensure that you eat healthy balanced foods throughout the week and also prevent waste. Only buy what you need to prepare the meals on your plan and do not pick up any impulse buys as these are likely to be the "naughty," stress-inducing foods. Also avoid shopping when hungry—it impacts on your food choices.

Constantly picking at food

Some people find that when they become stressed they begin to eat much more than they normally would. When a person is not stressed,

CASE STUDY:
Ricky Solanki, Director, Push Group

Being in charge of a small and rapidly growing business, I found myself under increasing pressure. We were taking on new clients and couldn't hire staff fast enough to deal with the additional workload, so I found myself working harder and for longer. I didn't take breaks, I would have a sandwich or a burger at my desk at lunchtime and used cups of tea and coffee and chocolate to get me through the day. I was always exhausted and at one point I had gotten so behind on my correspondence I found that I had 15,000 e-mails in my inbox! After some advice from a friend, I swapped the teas and coffees for water and green tea, the chocolates were exchanged for fruit and nuts and I made a point of eating a homemade lunch away from my desk. I found that the afternoon dips in energy that I used to suffer from disappeared and my productivity increased.

they only tend to eat food when they are hungry. The situation is very different under stress; in fact it is quite the opposite. Under stress, a person will eat when they are not even hungry and constantly pick at sugary or fatty snacks—keeping ourselves in a state of stress requires a lot of energy, hence we will crave energy-rich foods.

Eat well to relieve your stress

Eating healthy, nutritious food is a simple method for helping to relieve stress. When experiencing stress, it is vital to replenish your body's stores of B vitamins, vitamin E and essential minerals like magnesium to maintain a healthy immune system and revitalize your energy levels.

Good energy levels and a healthy immune system result in a higher resilience to stress. Similarly, certain foods can actively help to reduce stress levels:

- Fresh fruit and vegetables provide an array of vitamins and minerals that keep the body in top form. Vegetables also have a high fiber content, which is helpful in treating constipation—another long-term effect of stress.
- Oily fish such as salmon and mackerel contain omega fatty acids, which are extremely good for the heart and can protect you from heart diseases.
- Yogurts provide minerals including calcium, essential to maintain well-functioning nerve impulses. Calcium also contains lactobacillus, which is essential for maintaining healthy gut flora (micro organisms that help you to digest food properly).
- Nuts such as almonds are a nutritionally dense food that contain a number of important vitamins and minerals that can help you combat the effects of stress. As almonds are also somewhat high in calories, it's important to consume them in moderation (see

below). Regular nut consumption has been shown to help prevent heart disease, obesity and diabetes, which are also possible, negative consequences of too much stress.

20 STRESS-BUSTING FOODS:

1. **Nuts** are packed with magnesium, which helps keep cortisol levels low. A deficiency in magnesium is associated with feeling low and having a poor response to stress—all the more reason to get plenty of magnesium-rich foods like almonds or other nuts—eat a handful with some raisins as a snack. Nuts are high in calories, so if you're watching your weight, make sure not to eat more than a dozen a day. You can also get magnesium from lean meat, green vegetables and sunflower seeds.

2. **Broccoli** has folic acid, which aids stress reduction.

3. **Salmon** contains omega-3 fatty acids, which help brain cells to function more collaboratively, helping you to deal with stress more effectively.

4. **Dark chocolate** is by far the most potent endorphin-producing food on earth. However, you need to look for dark chocolate with a cocoa content of 70 percent or more. This is very different from the products that many of us consume believing we are eating chocolate—they are very low in the beneficial cocoa content and are mostly vegetable fat and sugar. A few squares of chocolate with 70 percent cocoa solids may give you a lift. However, do be aware that it does still contain sugar, so too much will have a negative effect and can also cause weight gain.

5. **Hot cocoa**. Warm drinks raise your body temperature—a feeling we associate with comfort—so it triggers a similar response in our brains. I am not referring to hot chocolate, which is packed with sugar; pure cocoa powder has no sugar in it and is not sweet, in fact it is quite bitter. Avoid adding sugar and if you need to sweeten it, use a little honey or agave syrup, which release into the blood more slowly than sugar and do not give your blood sugar the same spike followed by the crash.

6. **Green tea** is packed with theanine, which increases the brain's output of relaxation-inducing alpha waves and reduces the output of tension-making beta waves. Green tea does still contain caffeine, so be careful not to drink too much.

7. **Cold water**. Drink a glass, then go for a walk outside. The water gets your blood moving and the air invigorates you by stimulating the endorphins that de-stress you.

8. **Oatmeal**. Being a low glycemic index (GI) food, oats will provide you with sustained energy that will keep you going till lunchtime. And of all the cereals, oatmeal is the highest in protein, which leaves you feeling satisfied and fuller for longer than other breakfast cereals.

9. **Turkey**. Not only is turkey a healthy, low-fat source of protein, it also contains tryptophan from which we make the calming brain chemical serotonin.

10. **Oranges**. When under stress your vitamin C levels get depleted, resulting in susceptibility to illness.

Ensure you give your immune system a boost by eating plenty of vitamin C–rich foods, such as oranges, kiwis and strawberries.

11. **Bananas** are an excellent source of the mineral potassium, which your body needs to keep your blood pressure under control.

12. **White fish**. Eating white fish, such as pollack and haddock, can be particularly useful in helping us to get a good night's sleep and keep us happy. They are a great source of B vitamins, including B3, which is needed to make serotonin—a "feel-good" neurotransmitter found in the brain—and melatonin, a hormone which helps us to sleep.

13. **Asparagus**. This green vegetable is high in folic acid, which can help stabilize your mood. When you're stressed, your body releases hormones that affect your mood. Eating certain vitamins and minerals like folic acid and B vitamins can help keep your mood steady because they're needed to make serotonin, which is a chemical that directly affects mood in a positive way.

14. **Beef**. Even though beef often gets a bad name, it can be a great dinner option for a stressed-out family. Beef contains high levels of beneficial zinc and iron, plus B vitamins, which are known to help stabilize your mood. People think they should stay away from beef because some cuts contain a lot of fat, but it's very nutrient rich. Buy lean cuts if you're concerned about the fat content.

15. **Prunes**. Stress suppresses your immune system but you can boost it with antioxidants, and they don't

come much better than prunes. Prunes have the highest ORAC number (the measure of antioxidant activity) of any food. Don't fancy prunes? Don't worry, blueberries are nearly as good.

16. **Lettuce**. When the pressure is on, you don't want to be counting sheep into the wee small hours. Our Roman ancestors swore by the somnolent properties of lettuce and they were probably right—lettuce contains a compound related to opium and thus has sedative effects, so a lettuce sandwich before bedtime could help you drift off.

17. **Avocados**. The monounsaturated fats and potassium in avocados help lower blood pressure.

18. **Spinach**. A deficiency in magnesium can cause migraine headaches and a feeling of fatigue. One cup of spinach provides 40 percent of your daily needs.

19. **Sweet potatoes** can be particularly stress-reducing because they are naturally sweet, so they satisfy any urge you have to ingest carbohydrates and sweets when you are under a great deal of stress, yet they are packed full of beta-carotene and other vitamins, and the fiber helps your body to process the carbohydrates in a slow and steady manner.

20. **Camomile**. This gentle herb can relax muscles and have a calming influence on nervous irritability and anxiety. It can help with tension headaches, insomnia and irritable bowel syndrome, which are all symptoms of stress. Camomile supports refreshing and relaxing sleep and has a gentle sedative effect on the central nervous system.

Eat a rainbow

Many of the foods that are bad for you or highly processed are light in color and are best avoided. In fact, nature has done us a favor by coloring fruits and vegetables in a rainbow of colors, from the purple eggplant to the yellow banana. It's amazing to learn that there are over 350,000 edible plants on this planet, so don't get stuck preparing the same meals day after day. It's very important to vary your diet as your body responds well to a diverse range of foods—just as we get bored with eating the same types of food, our body gets stressed processing them. With a rainbow of colors on your plate comes a variety of minerals and vitamins, all of which will help to increase your resilience to stress. And they are delicious too!

Think "nervous"

Your nervous system is your body's center of operations and therefore it's important to develop and maintain a strong nervous system. This will help you in times of stress, as it will better equip you to respond to stressful situations without becoming overwhelmed. To do this, eat foods high in vitamins B and C and the minerals magnesium and zinc. Foods high in these vitamins and minerals include lean meat, nuts, seeds, fresh fruit and vegetables and oily fish. Pumpkin or sunflower seeds—or, even better, bananas—are great to snack on too. And wherever you can, do try and buy fresh and organic food. Frozen vegetables are a reasonable alternative as much of the nutritional content is retained during the freezing process. But avoid getting your vitamins and minerals from supplements wherever possible: your body processes vitamins and minerals more efficiently when they come in the form of food.

Avoid toxins

The saying "an apple a day keeps the doctor away" may have some truth in it—an apple can keep your immune system strong and healthy. However, if the apple that you are eating has come from a factory farm, then you could be consuming chemicals and pesticides alongside the healthy vitamins and minerals. In fact, toxic chemicals in the body can lead to poor health, illness and a decreased resilience to stress, thus undoing all the good work you did by eating the apple in the first place! In fact, certified organic food, which is not sprayed with chemicals, gives you more nutrition than nonorganic on a ratio of 1:30 (1 organic lettuce is as nutritionally valuable as 30 nonorganic lettuces). So eat organic wherever you can, as it will give your body what it needs to fight stress and its effects without adding chemicals that cause toxicity and stress.

Eat protein

Protein stimulates the release of glucagon, which mobilizes fat from storage and converts it into energy. This is why it's a good idea to eat protein with every meal and to eat it first. Protein makes you feel fuller, so eating it first helps control the amount you eat, and means that after your meal you are less likely to reach for the sugary snacks that can challenge an already stressed body.

Little and often

Small meals, eaten throughout the day, are the best way to improve your body's metabolism, so try not to go more than four hours without eating. As well as helping your body's metabolism, eating before you are hungry helps you to avoid overeating when you sit down for a meal. Whatever you do, don't skip meals. This will disrupt your body's sugar levels and slow down your metabolic rate, and you'll be much more susceptible to indulge in binge eating, which is itself stressful on the body.

MY PERSONAL ACTION PLAN

I promise myself I am going to improve my diet by taking these actions:

1. _____

2. _____

3. _____

4. _____

5. _____

Enter your commitments in your well-being journal to log your actions and progress.

CHAPTER 10

STEP 6:

Get moving to combat stress

When your body goes into a state of stress, it is expecting some kind of physical activity. It is anticipating having to run away or battle whatever has caused the stress, hence going into the fight-or-flight state. One way to take control of stress therefore is to give your body what it was anticipating—physical activity. Have you ever engaged in exercise or sports after a stressful day? How do you feel when you are finished?

ASSESS YOUR EXERCISE LEVELS

Do you get out of breath climbing the stairs?   Y/N

Do you NOT exercise to the point of perspiration
at least three times a week?   Y/N

When you bend down and then stand up, do you feel
light-headed or see spots?   Y/N

Do you feel exhausted after exercise instead of
exhilarated?   Y/N

Do you feel that exercise takes more from you
than it gives you?   Y/N

Do you resolve to exercise and then give up
without much effort?   Y/N
When you have free time, are you too tired to do
anything else but vegetate?   Y/N

If you answered yes to all or most of those questions, you need some
help. This chapter will give you a great start, with many practical
suggestions on improving your fitness and getting enough exercise to
build your resilience to stress.

EXERCISE AND STRESS RELIEF

Human beings were designed to be active and move, not to be sitting
statically on chairs for long periods of time; exercise is an essential
part of good body function. An extra bit of good news is that exercise
is also your shortest route to a feeling of well-being, relaxation and a
physical glow. Not only does it keep the heart healthy and get oxygen
into the system, being active can burn off the stress hormones, boost
your feel-good endorphins and take your mind off your daily worries.

Enhance your mood

Just as fight or flight has a potentially negative physiological effect
on the body, exercise has a positive one. It increases blood flow to
the body and brain and stimulates the nervous system in many positive ways. Most notably, exercise produces beta-endorphins, which
induce a natural "high" and will also improve your mood. Regular
exercise can increase self-confidence and lower the symptoms associated with mild depression and anxiety, and it can also improve your
sleep, which is often disrupted by stress, depression and anxiety. All

this can ease your stress levels and give you a sense of command over your body and your life. Whether you are building muscle or stamina, all types of exercise relax tense muscles and tissue. Tense muscles can strongly contribute to stress-related aches and pains, such as neck or back pains and headaches.

Forget your worries

Whatever form of exercise you decide to try, you will soon discover its major benefit is that it allows you to focus on something other than your problems. Not only do you become absorbed in what you are doing, the positive endorphins that exercise releases will also help you maintain a more positive outlook after you finish. If you are experiencing stress, physical activity can get you in the right state of mind to be able to identify the causes of your stress and find a solution and it will possibly be a solution in and of itself.

To deal with stress effectively you need to feel mentally strong, and robust exercise helps you to feel stronger and more in control. Even though it cannot make stress disappear, it may well reduce some of the emotional intensity that it can cause. It helps you to clear your thoughts and enables you to deal with your problems more effectively. It is after all what your body was expecting when you went into the fight-or-flight state.

The other major benefit is that exercise usually involves a change of scenery, either taking you to the gym, the park, a dojo, a boxing ring, the countryside, the beach, a scenic mountain, a biking trail or the streets in your neighborhood: all of these can be a pleasant alternative to the environments that caused your stress.

Let out your frustrations

Often when your bridge is overloaded and your experiences in life build up to the point of annoyance, frustration and anxiety, you can end up feeling stressed as a result of experiencing low-grade anger. Many high-intensity forms of exercise, such as boxing, martial arts, aerobics or spinning, can provide an effective release of these negative emotions. This allows you to turn potentially unhealthy emotions into motivation for increased health and well-being.

Look good

Another superficial, yet significant, benefit of exercise is that it will help you to lose weight, tone your body and maintain that healthy glow. You may find you experience a subtle but significant boost in your mood as your clothes look more flattering on you, and you project an aura of increased confidence and strength. This may appear shallow; however, it is important to note that stress and low self-esteem and low self-confidence are directly linked.

Social interaction

Exercise and physical activity often involve other people, and an added benefit is that working out with your friends is fun, motivating and helps you to relieve stress. It doesn't matter, really, what kind of

RUN OUTSIDE, NOT ON A TREADMILL

Going to the gym? Don't pound on a treadmill. This sort of monotonous indoor exercise actually causes the body to produce more of the stress hormone, cortisol, which will leave you feeling more stressed, not less. Running outside, on the other hand, will give you a much more interesting workout: the changing scenery will entertain your mind, fresh air will get into your lungs and you will produce less cortisol as a result.

exercise you do if you and your friends enjoy it, whether it's an aerobics or yoga class, spotting each other on weights, playing soccer in a local league or taking a walk through a beautiful piece of countryside. The benefits of having a buddy with you as you exercise are huge—he or she can help make the time go faster and in a more pleasant way, a healthy dose of competition can help both of you push yourselves harder and will help make your workout fun and enjoyable.

Resilience to stress

According to research, increased physical activity can be linked to lower physiological reactivity toward stress. That means that people who get more exercise are less likely to be affected by the stressful situations they experience. As we have seen, exercise is enormously beneficial on a range of levels, but what this research shows is that exercise can also protect you from stress that you may experience in the future, as well as lessening the stress that you may be experiencing right now. So get moving and enjoy the benefits of physical activity!

WHAT EXERCISE SHOULD YOU TRY?

All forms of exercise from yoga to pumping iron can provide stress-relieving benefit. Even if you are not an athlete (or possibly totally out of shape from years of camping on the couch), a little regular activity can take you a long way in helping you to manage your stress. The following forms of exercise have specific benefits for stress relief.

- **Yoga** is fantastic for health, well-being and flexibility and will also help you get into a relaxed, meditative state of mind.
- **Martial arts** are an effective way to develop self-discipline, become part of a community, release any pent-up tension and frustration

and even help you to feel safer, as you'll be better equipped to defend yourself in the event of an attack.

- **Swimming** is a brilliant way to get in shape. Most people find that water, with its cooling properties, is calming and relaxing, so it's a great way to relieve stress at the same time as getting in some exercise.
- **Walking** is something most people can do and is an easy and effective exercise to fit into a busy schedule. You can get off the bus or train a stop early, have a stroll at lunchtime, put young children in a stroller and go to the park. Walking with a friend and having a chat means that it doesn't even need to feel like you are exercising and it may also give you the added benefit of allowing you to get things off your chest. Walking alone allows you to think about things that are causing you stress and put them into perspective. It can also be a great moving meditation.

Competitive exercise adds an additional layer of benefit. Sports such as soccer, cricket, rugby and basketball enable you to push yourself harder and raise your game to a higher level than you may have been able to reach on your own. You could also try a sport with an opponent, such as tennis, badminton or golf, or even race against someone else by cycling, running or swimming. The added challenge helps to focus the mind and push yourself that little bit harder and in turn brings you additional stress-relieving benefits.

IS LIFE A SPRINT OR A MARATHON?

Think of a 100-meter sprinter. Think about his or her body. Sprinters are usually extremely muscular and stocky. During a race their bodies are usually very tight and tense; their teeth are gritted, their veins are bulging and they have looks of determination on their faces. What is their breathing like? A 100-meter sprinter wouldn't take a breath during the race; the breath would take time and energy, and the sprinter simply doesn't need to—the race is 10 seconds or less and anyone can hold the breath for that long.

Now I would like you to think of a marathon runner—somebody at the other end of the spectrum, engaged in the same activity, but whose approach is totally different. What kind of build does he or she have? Marathon runners are extremely lean; they carry no fat whatsoever. The state of their bodies during a race is completely different to that of a sprinter. They have very little tension in their bodies. Tense arms or shoulders or even a furrowed forehead require energy that could otherwise be used to aid their runs, so marathon runners hold their bodies in a fluid and relaxed state. What is their breathing like? Long-distance runners take slow, deep and rhythmical breaths. They breathe deep into their belly, maximizing the amount of oxygen they are inhaling, which in turn keeps them relaxed and helps to fuel their run.

Could marathon runners run a sprint? Yes, they could. Not at anywhere near the pace of a professional sprinter; however, they can and do sometimes sprint during a marathon, perhaps when jostling to overtake another competitor or to reach the finish line at the end of the race.

But what if, as the sprinter lined up on the starting blocks ready to run his 100-meter race, we informed him that we have decided we would like him to run a marathon at the same pace and intensity that he would run 100 meters. Could he do it? Well firstly, he couldn't hold his breath for that long! But, joking aside, the strain he would put on his body pushing himself that hard would eventually cause him to collapse and possibly even have a heart attack. He is not capable of running a marathon the same way he would run a sprint.

If we were to approach life like a sprinter, by pushing ourselves as hard as we can for as long as we can, we would face the same fate that he does. Not only would we not reach the finish line, chances are the illnesses of our lifestyle would strike us down long before we got there. Our approach to life should be that of a marathon runner: to develop a sustainable and maintainable pace, and to speed up when faced with a challenge for a stressful situation, always returning to our long-distance pace. Stress is useful for those short bursts and the sprinter uses stress constructively. However, if you want to keep going for extended periods of time, being relaxed will make it easier to do so. Life is a marathon distance, but every now and again you will be expected to break into a sprint. Far too many of us live our lives like 100-meter sprinters attempting to run a marathon; but develop the stamina and endurance of a long-distance runner and you will ensure that you happily and healthily keep yourself moving through the marathon that is your life.

PROGRESSIVE MUSCLE RELAXATION (PMR)

Our bodies respond to stress with muscular tension. It is thought to be one of the most common symptoms of stress. PMR is a stress-management technique that allows us to recognize and relieve this tension by contracting and then relaxing specific muscle groups in a systematic way. Concentrating on the technique also frees our minds from the problems or situations that caused the stress.

1. Begin by getting into a relaxed and comfortable position. Start by focusing on your breathing, taking slow, deep belly breaths.

2. Tighten a specific muscle group (see suggested order below) for about 5 to 10 seconds. Then quickly release the tension and relax the muscles for 15 to 30 seconds.

3. Be aware of the differences in the two different sensations. Enjoy the growing feelings of inner comfort as you release any tension.

4. You will be working on tensing and relaxing these muscle groups in a specific order.

Here is a suggested order:

1. Right foot
2. Right lower leg and foot
3. Entire right leg
4. Left foot
5. Left lower leg and foot
6. Entire left leg
7. Right hand
8. Right forearm and hand
9. Entire right arm
10. Left hand
11. Left forearm and hand
12. Entire left arm
13. Abdomen
14. Neck and shoulders
15. Face

Some people start at the feet and work up while others start at the head and work down. Do whichever feels most comfortable to you. End the session by again taking a few minutes to relax, deep breathe and enjoy yourself. Open your eyes and do a few stretches. Wiggle your toes and fingers. You will feel refreshed!

There are several different ways to do this exercise, and remember, there is no right or wrong way to approach this. The best way to learn this technique is to practice it on a daily basis! Plan to do PMR twice per day. Each session takes about 10 to 15 minutes.

Tips

- Find a quiet place to practice the exercise without music or interruptions. Keep the lights low.
- Wear loose clothing and take off your shoes.
- It is best to do PMR before eating, smoking or drinking alcohol.
- Do not hold your breath during the exercises. Get into the habit of breathing in while you tense a muscle and breathing out while you release the tension.
- To tense your hand, make a fist.
- When tensing your facial muscles, squeeze your eyes shut. You can also clench your teeth and pull back the corners of your mouth.
- Shrug your shoulders and pull them into your neck to tense them.
- Use PMR to fall asleep at night.
- As you perfect your technique, you will learn to quickly recognize the feeling of tension and stress

building in your muscles and then be able to quickly release it on command.

- Be aware that PMR should not be used if you have heart problems or high blood pressure without first consulting your healthcare provider. If you have had any serious injuries, muscle spasms or back pain, you should also talk with your doctor before trying PMR.

MY PERSONAL ACTION PLAN

I promise myself I am going to improve my fitness and exercise levels by taking these actions:

1. _____

2. _____

3. _____

4. _____

5. _____

Enter your commitments in your well-being journal to log your actions and progress.

CHAPTER 11

STEP 7:

Adopt a positive mindset

Being in control of your thoughts vastly increases your ability to find solutions to challenging situations and deal more effectively with stress and pressure. It better equips you for even the most stressful of situations. Master your mind and you'll never wonder how to deal with stress again.

ASSESS YOUR MINDSET

Do you often find yourself worrying about all that could go wrong?   Y/N

Do you consider yourself a glass-half-empty kind of person?   Y/N

Do little things often cause exaggerated emotional reactions?   Y/N

Do you find constant mind chatter distracts you?   Y/N

When stressed do you feel confused?   Y/N

Have you ever become forgetful or suffered from a mental block when stressed?   Y/N

Do you control your mind or does it control you?   Y/N

If you answered yes to all or most of those questions, you need some help. This chapter will give you a great start, with many practical suggestions on mastering your mind to reduce the impact of stress.

ALTER YOUR BODY, CHANGE YOUR MIND, DE-STRESS

Daily mental thought training is easier and far more pleasurable than you can imagine. Experience it for only a couple of days and you'll understand firsthand that the power you have over your thoughts is the ultimate power. In the previous chapter, I introduced the concept of changing your psychology by changing your physiology. The majority of people would agree that our state of mind can have a significant impact on our physical state. If you believe a situation is overwhelming and that you cannot cope with the stress, you will convince yourself of that viewpoint, making the situation much harder to handle. However, can the same be said of the opposite? Can you change your state of mind through shifting your physiology? Of course you can! What researchers into stress have discovered is that by changing certain aspects of your body, your thoughts and feelings can be changed too. Here are some simple ways to change your mood.

Eliminate stress with a smile!

Let's think about the power of a simple smile. You may believe that smiling must be triggered by what you are thinking and how you feel, not that the physical act of smiling will change your mindset. However, the truth is that if you choose to smile, you will automatically feel happier. Give it a go right now. Just take the corners of your mouth and curl them upward until you feel a broad smile forming. Notice the changes in how you feel. You will immediately start to feel different. Your physiology has a direct impact on your psychology. If you find yourself feeling down and sad, force yourself to smile, and you will notice the change in your thought patterns and emotions. Remember that the quickest way to change your psychology is to change your physiology. The reverse is also true—change your physiology to quickly shift your psychological state

Stand up straight

Bad posture can also have a negative impact on your emotional state. If you are slouching or sitting slumped in your chair, you will struggle to get yourself into an optimum state. By standing upright or sitting straight with your spine erect, your body is communicating to your mind that it needs to align its state. This is the magic of "matter of mind."

Act as if . . .

When you experience a stressful event, the first thing to do is step back, take a slow, deep breath and analyze the situation. Then you can forcibly change your thoughts using your physical state. As the saying goes: "fake it till you make it!" Simply start by pretending to be who or what you would like to be. If you feel down and stressed, begin by acting like someone that is happy and relaxed. If you feel tired and lethargic, start acting like someone who has an abundance of energy. Think about how people you aspire to be like would act and emulate them. This is the catalyst that changes your state of mind and your thought patterns and, in turn, impacts your physical state. Before you know it you will have powerful momentum for making the positive changes required to shift your life in a new direction.

Get moving

The breathing exercises in Chapter 7 are also another way for your physical state to alter your mental state. Exercise and yoga, both of which help your breathing, also have the same effects.

THINK POSITIVE

I've noticed in many people who attend my workshops that it's hard for them to conceive that they can change their thoughts easily, but there are simply countless ways to alter your mindset (I have written an entire book on the subject). Of course, most people are skeptics, especially when I tell them I simply "choose to be happy."

Harness the power of the mind

Everyone has a little voice in their mind that verbalizes their thoughts. Your little voice has the potential to be very powerful and also some-times very loud! It connects with your subconscious mind and protects and empowers you by providing important messages and answers to challenges that you are facing. Acknowledge your little voice and what it has to say, then ask yourself:

- Is this thought useful and/or helpful?
- What would be a thought that would serve you better?
- Is my little voice providing me with a warning message that I need to pay attention to?
- Is there a positive intention or purpose behind the message from my little voice?

Focusing on what your little voice has to say can give you the answers to any challenges you may be facing and allow you to respond in a more positive and resourceful manner. You may also find, however, that your little voice can sabotage you and hold you back. Even though it may lead to a negative result, this sabotage may well have a positive intention. It doesn't want you to get hurt, to experience pain or to fail, so it convinces you not to even attempt things that could lead to a negative outcome.

It's important to know that you have the power to turn your little voice into your best ally, your partner in success and achievement.

You can also change its impact when it isn't serving you; simply turn down the volume, adjust the pitch and tone.

Just imagine your little voice is talking down to you, telling you that you are not good enough, that you are going to fail miserably or asking you who the hell you think you are. Now make your little voice sound like Mickey Mouse or Homer Simpson. When it sounds ridiculous it cannot hold the same power over you. Do remember it's *your* voice and *you* have full control over it. You have the ability to change what it is saying and how it says it. These techniques put you back in control of your thoughts and reactions to situations.

Erase negative thoughts

Nothing is certain in life—except the fact that as we move through it we will encounter change, good and bad. Moving house, for example, is something that is seen as inherently stressful, but you can heighten or lessen your stress levels by the way that you perceive such an event.

Take Joe, for example. Joe has decided to take a new job in another part of the country. He's not looking forward to it: "What if our house never sells, I won't be able to afford a big enough place for my family." He is worried that he's made the wrong decision: "What if my job turns out to be rubbish? Would that make my wife leave me?" "What if my kids don't make friends at their new school? Will they hate me for taking them out of a place they knew?"

Joe is thinking negatively and the normal flow of his mind is disrupted. Rather than concentrating on the task at hand, Joe is distracting himself with the worst possible scenarios. He is making stressful situations—a new job and a house move—worse just by adopting a negative mindset.

I'm not saying that Joe's worries aren't normal. But by looking at them negatively, he's focusing on problems, not solutions. Here's how he might think of his worries in a positive way:

- "What if our house doesn't sell? Well then, we will see if we can rent it out for a time. That would help with our income in the new place. Meanwhile, I've taken a look around our new city, and there are nice-looking areas with houses we can afford."
- "What if my job turns out to be rubbish? I think that's going to be unlikely, as I researched the company before I took on the job. However, if it turns out that the job isn't for me, I will discuss with my wife what we should do."
- "What if my kids don't make friends at their new school? My wife and I will make sure that they go to lots of after-school and week-end activities where they are bound to find other kids they like."

See the difference? The worries are still there, but by thinking about them positively, Joe can find solutions. This means that he can look forward to his new life with his family, rather than dread things that may not occur.

Take heed of your emotions

Your emotions can cloud your sense of judgment, and in order for you to focus your mind correctly, you need to control them. When you are angry, depressed, stressed, etc., it is much harder to concentrate on anything. However, even though they force us to make mistakes, it is always important to listen to your emotions, as sometimes they are trying to tell you that something is wrong inside the body. Controlling your emotional state is similar to dealing with negative thoughts.

- Upon an emotion occurring: take a deep breath, relax and step back from the situation.
- Recognize the emotions you are experiencing and think about what is causing this emotional reaction. When you have figured out the cause of the emotion, take action to diminish its impact.

By taking these steps, you can begin to reduce the stress you inflict on your body just by managing and containing your emotions. When you start to feel your emotions welling up and beginning to impact your state, that is the time to do something about it. If suppressed and allowed to linger, these bottled-up emotions can lead to far more serious stress- and health-related problems.

Relax your mind

If you want to have a clear and focused mind, relaxation is one of the most important things to do. Often we work long hours without rest in order to get a job done. If you do this infrequently, you will inflict stress on the body, but the effects will be minimal. If, on the other hand, this continues for extended periods of time, you are likely to suffer stress-related illnesses, which can impact you severely, causing serious long-term damage to your health and well-being.

In order to prevent this, it is important that you take the time to relax on a regular basis and allow your mind to turn off. Remember, a sprinter can run only for short distances before he has to rest and recover. There are many ways to relax your mind:

- **Meditation** is a perfect opportunity to gain some peace of mind and disconnect from your physical environment. Spending even 10 to 15 minutes quieting the mind and focusing on the present moment makes us more relaxed and more effective decision makers.
- **Sleep** is vital for the body to recover but it also puts the mind into a relaxed state. Maintaining good sleep patterns is paramount to remaining focused and energized in your daily life as well as better equipping you to cope with any stress-related challenges that you are likely to experience (for more about the importance of sleep see Chapter 6).

- **Hobbies and sports** give you something to focus on outside of your work and the daily routine of life, and can be hugely beneficial in relaxing the mind. They give you something pleasurable to look forward to.

CASE STUDY:
Neil Shah, mastering my little voice

I spent most of my life struggling with my little voice. As a child and a teenager I had low self-esteem and self-confidence and my voice was constantly reminding me why I was not good enough, why I was likely to fail and why I was unlikely to achieve success. When I really pushed myself to my limits, my little voice seemed only to get louder and more aggressive.

The first couple of times I ran the marathon, even though I was physically prepared, my little voice seemed to get the better of me, telling me, "You're not good enough; you're tired; you can't do this; who do you think you are trying to run the marathon?" It always seemed to get the better of me, and the mental exhaustion I suffered as a result was more of a challenge than the physical tiredness.

For the last marathon I ran I spent as much time preparing my mind as I did my body. I did all I could to ensure that my little voice did not sabotage my attempt. I set myself a goal of finishing the race in less than 5 hours (my previous personal best was 5 hours 45 minutes).

Initially my marathon went well, then at 15 miles I had to slow down to a run-then-walk pattern. The little voice kicked in with its usual stories. By 20 miles I worked out that I'd fallen so behind that I wouldn't break the 5-hour barrier. I turned down the volume of my little voice and gave him a cartoon-like squeak. He stopped affecting me so I decided just to go for it, push through the pain barrier and pick up my pace. Then I came across Matt, a marathon pacemaker (someone who runs just for other people to set their pace to). I informed him of my goal and he suggested I stick with him as he was on track to finish in under 5 hours. Matt was running fast and I had to dig deep, ignore the pain and use every last ounce of reserve energy I had. There could be no bathroom or water stops. I simply had to push myself and run faster than I had at the start of the race. I had never been able to do anything like that. I was raising money for a tiger charity and I visualized a tiger walking free and safe through the jungle, which seemed to help. Now it wasn't about me, it was about the tigers.

Then things changed. Matt turned to me and said: "Listen, mate, there's just under 2 miles to go and even at this pace you're not going to make it in under five hours. Maybe 5:02 or 5:03. So if you want to break 5, you're going to have to sprint."

I didn't even hesitate and simply shifted up another gear. At this point, the race was no longer a physical challenge; it was a mental and emotional battle. So I gave myself all the help I could. I kept chanting as loud as I could, "I can do this! I can do this!" over and over. Some people gave me strange looks, but others—and I'm amazed by how many—called back "Yes, you can!

Yes, you can!" With that cheering, I found the strength to push harder than ever before. The blood was pumping through me and suddenly there was the finish line. The clock above it said that I had seconds to go before 5 hours. I let out an enormous roar and gave it all I had . . . And then I felt really light-headed. I don't remember what happened next; I just know that I was meters from my goal and my mind went blank. The next thing I knew, I opened my eyes and there was bright white light surrounding me. I was aware of how still I was. Was I floating? I felt woozy but there was a weight pushing down on my chest. My first thought was "I'm dead." But slowly I raised my hand to my heart to see if it was beating, and found a medal hanging around my neck. I was also wearing an oxygen mask. I suddenly realized that I was in the hospital tent, very much alive, and I was grasping the proof that I'd finished my marathon!

A passing doctor told me I had keeled over unconscious as I crossed the line. I was exhausted and dehydrated, but otherwise okay. Obviously this wasn't the ideal outcome, as I would have liked to remember finishing the race, and I wouldn't recommend this approach, as you could cause yourself serious harm by pushing yourself too hard. However, this is a perfect example of how important your mindset can be in helping you achieve your goals.

I still didn't know whether I had broken the 5-hour barrier when I logged on to the marathon Web site, so I was thrilled to discover my time was 4 hours, 58 minutes and 58 seconds! I was 1 minute and 2 seconds under my target.

> That experience not only taught me how important it is to minimize the negative impact of our little voices, but also that it's vital to replace them with positive affirmations.

USING SELF-HYPNOSIS TO REDUCE STRESS

Hypnosis can be described as a situation where we naturally focus inward to access memories, feelings, intuition and direction while being less aware of our external world. It is a natural state of being that we experience more or less every day of our lives and it is this natural (subconcious) world of ours that opens up possibilities for us to explore, so that we can understand and improve our lives in whatever way we want to. There is so much fear and mystery around the word "hypnosis," but today we have the opportunity to dispel the myths and misconceptions around this fascinating and yet natural state of relaxation.

When we access memories, daydream or are engrossed in a book, we are in actual fact experiencing a light form of trance, or hypnosis. There are times when we take automatic actions without being aware of them, for example driving from one place to another. The subconscious takes over so it is driving on "automatic pilot." This is also a form of hypnosis. Yet for various reasons, many of us have a fear of the subconscious mind. One popular myth is that it is full of repressed desires and behaviors that either we are unaware of, or that these influences might suddenly appear in an uncontrollable way. When considering this idea logically, it must be faulty, because all of our natural actions and responses are due to the working of the subconscious. Walking, talking and our heart beating are all subconscious actions, which are happening continuously without us taking any notice of them. The subconscious mind must, therefore, be accepted as a vital part of our being. Without it we could not exist! Other actions such as natural reflexes and intuition are due to the complex and vital work of the subconscious. Even when we are fearful of something, or in physical pain, these are warnings from our subconscious that something should be looked at or some action taken to change the situation in order that equilibrium can be achieved again.

So let us consider that our subconscious is our greatest friend. When you really accept this concept you will be surprised at how much easier it is to gain and understand so many more of our innate benefits and skills. It has been suggested that we use or are aware of only around 3 percent of our subconscious—just imagine how much more there is for us to discover!

Exercises to achieve self-hypnosis

There are numerous ways to achieve this natural state of relaxation, so here are some examples. Know that you are always 100 percent correct whatever you encounter, so just let go and enjoy your experience.

Defocusing

Sitting comfortably, become aware of a spot or tiny point in front of you. Focus on it, allowing your breathing to become calmer. Focus until it becomes difficult to do so, by now it will be easy to close your eyes naturally and drift into a deeper state of relaxation. You can do this for as little as five minutes or as long as your schedule allows. The more time you spend in this state the better.

Pleasant memory technique

Sitting comfortably with your eyes closed, becoming aware of the natural relaxation on your outward breath, imagine you are walking along your pathway in life, and there are turnings off it, which lead you to a very pleasant memory or experience that you remember well. Take one of them. Heighten the experience by being aware of your five senses and relive it, enhancing it if necessary to achieve or find whatever you wish. Return along the same pathway to the main pathway, bringing the good feelings and experiences with you. Then open your eyes.

Relaxing in the sunshine technique

Sitting comfortably, imagine you are sunbathing and receiving just the right amount of sunlight, while being aware of the relaxation on your outward breath. Imagine the wonderful warm rays lighting up your mind and freeing your mind of limitations, so that you can learn or understand something or achieve whatever is appropriate for you.

Guided imagery

Guided imagery is a form of self-hypnosis that has been associated with positive stimulation of the immune system. Positive suggestion is used to release negative self-image, assist in creating and achieving goals and as a natural way to relieve physical, mental and emotional stress. The method can be used to treat stress-related illnesses such as high blood pressure and insomnia. It is a terrific way to reduce stress and to work through those day-to-day challenges. It's simple, low-tech and effective: all you need is your imagination and a few minutes to yourself.

Begin by closing your eyes and taking deep, measured breaths. Imagine that you are in beautiful surroundings—either a place you have visited or a place you conjure up from your imagination. Focus on bringing all the elements of the scene to life: the colors you see, the sounds you hear, the smells you detect, the aromas and the taste. How does your body feel in this environment? Is it warm or cool? Are you alone or with others? Bring the images into focus and try to "stay in the scene" for at least 5 minutes. Practice this exercise for a few minutes every day or use it whenever you're stressed.

Using affirmations to reduce stress

Positive affirmations can be a powerful tool in transforming the negative power of your little voice and turning it into a positive, motivational and affirming little voice. Here are some affirmations you can use that are designed to reduce stress, increase feelings of personal power and awaken your mind to possibilities for change, helping you to fulfill your potential.

Use some of these affirmations or create your own:

- I am calm
- I am relaxed
- I am confident
- I am stress-free
- Challenges help me grow
- Challenges bring opportunities
- I have a proper perspective
- I am in charge
- I am in control
- I am at peace with myself
- I am at peace with the world around me
- I like exercise
- I exercise
- I like relaxation
- I relax regularly
- I am tranquil
- I forgive others
- I am at ease
- I am calm
- I am relaxed
- I breathe deeply
- I remain calm

- I can choose a positive frame of mind
- I can handle whatever comes my way
- I have balance in my life
- I can accomplish anything
- I create inner peace
- I am strong
- My intentions create my reality
- I make healthy choices
- I create positive change
- I am calm under pressure
- I choose happiness
- I choose healthy relationships

MY PERSONAL ACTION PLAN

I promise myself I am going to adopt a more positive mindset by taking these actions:

1. _____

2. _____

3. _____

4. _____

5. _____

Enter your commitments in your well-being journal to log your actions and progress.

CHAPTER 12

STEP 8:

Be the master of your time

Time management is a stress-management technique. If you fail to master your time, you get overwhelmed, you get stressed and your productivity and efficiency diminish.

ASSESS HOW WELL YOU MANAGE YOUR TIME

Are you always running late?	Y/N
Do you rarely take breaks during the day?	Y/N
Do you eat your lunch at your desk while working?	Y/N
Do you frequently have to work late to catch up on your workload?	Y/N
Do you often check work e-mails in the evening and on weekends?	Y/N
Do you feel that there are not enough hours in the day?	Y/N

If you answered yes to all or most of those questions, you need some help. This chapter will give you a great start, with many practical suggestions for improving how you manage your time, thus ensuring that you are more productive and efficient and as a result less stressed.

TIME MANAGEMENT

Good time management is essential if you are to handle a heavy workload without excessive stress. Time management helps you to reduce long-term stress by giving you direction when you have too much work to do. It puts you in control of where you are going, and helps you to increase your productivity. By being efficient in your use of time, you should enjoy your current work more, and should find that you are able to maximize the time outside work to relax and to enjoy life.

Poor time management is a major cause of stress. I'm sure we have all had the feeling that there is too much to do and not enough time. We can start to feel panicky and anxious and lose focus. It's important to note that you can have this feeling even if there's hardly anything to do at all. Many people who suffer from poor time management suffer from what I call the "freeze" state. As we have seen on page 18, the "fight-or-flight" state is driven by the part of the brain called the medulla oblongata. This part of your brain is set up for survival, and is designed to focus on the imminent danger and to force you to act or react to do what's necessary to remove yourself from the danger. It cannot focus particularly well on multiple challenges and can become overloaded when you have too much on your bridge. When that happens, it is literally incapacitated and you will shut down. You are incapable of taking any action. Have you experienced a time such as this when you had a lot on your plate, but you found yourself frozen like a deer in the headlights?

Symptoms of stress caused by poor time management

- Irritability and mood swings. People around you may notice this first (i.e., friends, family, colleagues, etc.).
- Tiredness and fatigue. Most people don't even notice this as they accept that being tired is part of life!
- Inability to focus or concentrate. Do you ever feel like you are just trying to get yourself through the day?
- Mental blocks, memory lapses and forgetfulness. Forgetting what you watched on TV last night, what you had for breakfast, etc.
- Lack of, or loss of, sleep. As we have seen in Chapter 6, this can affect your day, your mood and your body.
- Physical ailments and disorders such as headaches, rashes, nervous tics, cramps, etc.
- At worst, withdrawal and depression.

Also, when you have failed to manage your time you may be unclear about what is important and end up working on the things that are put in front of you or reacting to demands made by others rather than doing the work that needs to be done.

MANAGE YOUR TIME MORE EFFECTIVELY

As long as you commit to taking action, time management is easy. Simple steps can result in more effective management of your time. These can include:

- better planning
- better prioritizing
- delegating tasks to others
- controlling your environment

- understanding yourself and identifying what you will change about your habits, routines and attitudes.

Plan

Planning is another key step in successfully managing your time. The next step is protecting the planned time. If you find yourself saying you "do not have time," chances are you have not planned, or have failed to protect, planned time. If you plan what to do and when to do it, and then stick to the plan, you will have the time that you need. If you have demands placed upon you by others, particularly at work—e.g., other departments, managers, customers, etc.—time management requires diplomatically managing the expectations of others. Planning can also be disrupted by modern technologies: an e-mail pings into your inbox, you receive a telephone call, a text message . . . These distract you and you may then end up responding to the issue as it is in front of you, even if it is not the most valuable use of your time. These technologies can prevent us from following our well-structured plan for our day.

Prioritize

An effective way of ensuring that you use your time most effectively is to prioritize your tasks. Start by making a list of the things that you need to do, ensuring that you list them in terms of genuine importance. Be clear about what you need to do personally and what can be delegated to others. Then note what is urgent and needs to be done immediately, then what can be done tomorrow, next week, next month, etc. At the end of each day write down the most important tasks you have to do tomorrow and number them in order of importance. You may waste a lot of time doing unimportant or unnecessary tasks, so prioritizing your day and doing the important jobs first (although you will also need to create time buffers to deal with unexpected emergencies) will help to avoid stress due to time wasted. The unimportant tasks can wait, and can often disappear altogether, leaving you time to do other things. Do not put off the unpleasant or unenjoyable tasks. Every time we think about them we cause ourselves stress. Give an unpleasant task a high priority and do it first. Learn how to say no. This simple and yet extremely effective skill will prevent too much pressure building up in the future (for more about this technique, see Chapter 14).

A pivotal shift in attitude when considering time management is to concentrate on results, not on the activity itself. The prioritization grid on pages 138–39 will help with this. When you begin work, start with the number 1 priorities. Stay on them until they are all completed. Recheck your priorities and then start on the number 2s. If any number 1 or 2 tasks take all day, never mind, stick with them as long as they are the most important ones. If you don't finish all your tasks, you probably couldn't with any other method, and without some system you'd probably not even decide which one was the most important one. Also in turn you may get distracted by lower priority tasks and also jump from activity to activity. Make this a habit every working day. The source of the stress and anxiety—an overwhelming and unmanageable list of tasks—will become realistic and manageable and spread out over a more sensible time frame. You will notice that some items will be delegated to others or removed from the list altogether with the realization that they are unnecessary or unimportant. Use the following prioritization grid to sort your tasks in order of importance. Once you have prioritized your tasks, if you find you have anything in quadrant 4, ask yourself, if it is not urgent and not important, do you need to do it at all?

Prioritization grid

	Urgent	Not urgent
Important	1—Do immediately	2—Plan to do
	• Actual emergencies and major crisis issues	• Planning and preparation
	• Serious urgent complaints	• Scheduling and planning project-related activities
	• Significant demands for information from superiors or customers	• Research and investigative activities
	• Any activities that have an imminent deadline	• Networking
	• Scheduled meetings and appointments	• Relationship building
	• Time-sensitive reports	• Brainstorming and creativity
	• People needs (e.g., family, child-related issues, staff issues, etc.)	• Modeling, designing, testing
	• Problem resolution and firefighting	• Anticipative and preventative measures/activities or communication
		• Identifying new opportunities, need for change and new direction
		• Developing or creating strategy
		• Recreation

- **Urgent and important:** First make sure that these tasks are genuinely important and need to be done straightaway. Tackle each task according to how urgent it is—if two tasks seem equally urgent, talk through each task with the person who gave it to you. It might be that the deadline on one is more flexible than the other.
- **Break down big tasks into bite-sized chunks:** Have time slots and logical progressions for each chunk.

	Urgent	Not urgent
Not important	3—Reject (diplomatically) • Trivial and "dumped" requests from others • Perceived but noncritical "emergencies" • Unexpected disturbances and interruptions • Misunderstandings or miscommunications perceived as complaints • Irrelevant distractions (e.g., Facebook) • Pointless routines or activities • Duplication of effort • Unnecessary double-checking • Whims and tantrums of others	4—Stop immediately • Unnecessary and unchallenged routines • "Comfort" activities: video games, Internet surfing, social media, cigarette breaks • Idle chat and gossip • Unnecessary and irrelevant social and domestic communications • Silly, pointless e-mails and text messages • Pointlessly interrupting others • Reading nonsense or irrelevant material • Unnecessary adjusting: tidying, updating equipment, systems, screensavers, etc. • Overly long breaks and canteen or kitchen visits • Aimless, passive daydreaming • Aimless travel and driving • Unnecessary and pointless shopping

• **Keep people informed:** Talk through your to-do list with the people involved, so that they understand how you are prioritizing your time in a productive, efficient and effective way.

- **Plan to do:** These tasks are usually the ones that are most critical to the long-term success of a project, but often, perhaps because of "firefighting" urgent problems belonging to other people (see Reject [diplomatically]), they often get pushed to one side. But as these tasks often involve activities that are vital to the future success of a project, such as planning, strategy, brainstorming new ideas and determining aims and objectives, they should become a priority. Allocate time to these tasks, and try to do them in a place where you will be free from any interruptions or distractions.

- **Reject (diplomatically):** Look at each demand on your time with a discerning eye and query the real importance of demands made on you, even by your boss or senior figures. Make sure you manage people's expectations and sensitivities accordingly and when appropriate, learn to say no (see Chapter 14); be prepared to explain why you are declining the task. You might suggest another way of achieving what they need. This could involve delegating to another person or changing the task itself. Help and support others to manage their own time and priorities, so they don't end up putting their load onto your bridge.

- **Stop immediately:** People suffering from time stress may focus on these activities as a form of escapism or denial. These activities are not tasks, they are habitual comforters that provide a refuge from the effort of discipline and proactivity. A group or whole department all doing a lot of this quadrant's activity creates a nonproductive and ineffective organizational culture. These activities have no positive outcomes, and are therefore demotivating. Consider why you do these things, and if there's a deeper root cause, address it. The best method for ceasing these activities, and for removing temptation to gravitate back to them, is to have a clear structure or schedule of tasks for each day, which you should create in quadrant 2.

MYTHS ABOUT TIME MANAGEMENT

- **Myth: Planning my time is more time wasted.**
  Truth: Actually, research suggests completely the opposite. Knowing how you should be spending your time and what you should be spending it on is the first step toward effective time management. Begin by clarifying your priorities. Immediately you will find that you use your time more effectively.

- **Myth: If there is not enough time to get done what needs to get done, then I have a time-management problem.**
  Truth: A time-management problem is not using your time to your fullest advantage, to get done what you want to get done. You are not making the most effective use of your time.

- **Myth: The busier I am, the more I am getting done.**
  Truth: Be warned—you may just be a busy fool! You may be doing only what's urgent (quadrant 3), and not what's important and urgent (quadrant 1).

- **Myth: I feel very hassled and stressed, so I must have a time-management problem.**
  Truth: You may not have a time-management problem—first you should make sure that this really is the issue by being clear about what needs to be done and if it is actually getting done or not.

TIME ROBBERS

A time robber is literally anything or anyone that steals your time. This is a major cause of time stress. Time robbers are a problem when trying to manage your time effectively, as they are generally unexpected or unscheduled interruptions. Dealing with time robbers is ultimately a problem-solving exercise consisting of a logical step-by-step analysis of what the problem actually is. It is also necessary to define the level of control. A useful device for ascertaining this level is the TOP principle. Ask yourself: is the problem . . .

- **T**otally within my control?
- **O**utside of my control?
- **P**artially within my control (and if so, which part is within and which part is outside)?

If the problem is totally outside of your control, then there is absolutely no point in attempting to solve it. Use the table below to better understand your time robbers and understand what power you have to do something about them. This way you can focus on the things that are within your control and delegate or ignore the things that are out of your control.

What is your time robber/issue?	T	O	P
1)			
2)			
3)			

Conclusion and action(s)
1)
2)
3)

KEY PRINCIPLES OF GOOD TIME-STRESS MANAGEMENT

- Learn your signs and symptoms of time stress. Ask your friends, family or colleagues how you act when under stress or when your bridge is overloaded with demands. They may be able to tell you what they observe when you're overstressed or under pressure.

- Most people feel that they are stressed and/or they poorly manage their time. Verify that you really do have a problem by completing the questionnaire at the beginning of this chapter. What is it about the way you manage time and stress that makes you feel you have a problem?

- Don't work under the mistaken assumption that more work equals more happiness. The quality of work that you do is more important than the quantity, so concentrate on results, not on being busy.

- One of the major benefits of planning your time more effectively is feeling that you're in control, in turn allowing you to feel more empowered.

- Book a one-hour meeting with yourself every day—if you have any unexpected calls or visitors, this hour is your time buffer. If you don't have any unexpected demands on your time, I am sure you will find a way of using that hour!

TIME-MANAGEMENT EXERCISES

The following exercises are designed to help you become more effective at managing and planning your time. Like with any form of exercise, the more you practice the easier it gets, so try to make these part of your regular routine and eventually they will become second nature.

Exercise 1: Become a better estimator

Pick a few tasks that you will be working on over the next few days. Jot down your estimate of how long it is likely to take to complete each task. When you are actually working on the task keep a note of how long you spend on each one. Then when all the tasks are complete compare your estimates with actual time spent.

- **Within 20 percent of your estimate?**
  Well done—you seem to be clear about how long things are likely to take and you will find it easier to schedule your time and activities without becoming overwhelmed and behind schedule and missing deadlines. This will also help you to avoid having too much to do and not enough time.

- **Above or below 20 percent of your estimate?**
  If you were above or below the 20 percent mark, look for reasons why you might have over- or underestimated the time required. Use your insights to adjust your estimates on future tasks.

Repeat regularly for one month to improve your ability to estimate required task times, and in turn improve your ability to plan and schedule your time accurately.

Exercise 2: Power time log

You probably are already aware of what time of the day you work best. Whether you're a morning, afternoon or evening person, the time of the day when you're most productive and focused is what we will call your "power time."

- For a week, pick a two-hour slot within your power time. Every 15 minutes throughout that slot, jot down what you were doing in the last quarter of an hour.
- At the end of the week, review and analyze the log. Calculate how much of your power time you devoted to quadrant 1 and 2 tasks.

Many of us spend our power time focused on quadrant 3 or 4 activities. Plan and schedule your future quadrant 1 and 2 tasks into your power time.

MY PERSONAL ACTION PLAN

I promise myself I am going to improve my time management by taking these actions:

1. _____

2. _____

3. _____

4. _____

5. _____

Enter your commitments in your well-being journal to log your actions and progress.

CHAPTER 13

STEP 9:

Don't be a slave to technology—master it

The impact of technology on our stress levels was really put into perspective for me recently. I was speaking at a human resources (HR) conference about workplace stress. The attendees were senior HR professionals (directors and managers) from large European companies. My slot was just before the morning break, which was the first break of the conference. I came off the stage and needed to rush to the station as I had a train to catch back to London. I ran to the bathroom before I left and it seems that, as it was the first break, so had everybody else—all 12 of the urinals were being used and there were about 5 or 6 people waiting. As I looked up at the people that were "taking a leak," I was astounded at what I saw. In fact, if it had been appropriate, I would have taken a picture as it would have made such a powerful visual to accompany this story. Each and every single one of those gentlemen were on their phones while peeing! Some were looking at the screen, possibly checking e-mails or texts, some had their phone to their ears, possibly listening to voicemail, and one was actually on the phone to his office, barking orders at an underling! It really did put things into perspective, when witnessing a group of busy professionals who didn't even have a minute to use the bathroom in peace! A sprinter who never rests or recovers after racing would soon run out of steam, and the "always on" technology is denying us the valuable recovery time required to ensure we are as well equipped as possible to cope with stress when it arises. Let's call technology-related stress "tech-stress."

ASSESS THE IMPACT TECHNOLOGY HAS ON YOUR STRESS LEVELS

Do you own a smartphone (iPhone, BlackBerry, Android etc.)?   Y/N

Do you spend your day working in front of a computer?   Y/N

Have you ever checked your e-mails, social media, text messages, etc., while on the toilet?   Y/N

Have you ever checked your e-mails, social media, text messages, etc., in bed?   Y/N

Do you feel panicky and anxious if you don't have your phone on you or if the battery is dead?   Y/N

Since you picked up this book to read, have you at any point stopped to check e-mails, social media, text messages, etc.?   Y/N

If you answered yes to all or most of those questions, you need some help. This chapter will give you a great start, with many practical suggestions on improving your mastery of technology so it doesn't become a cause of stress in your life.

IS TECHNOLOGY STRESSING YOU OUT?

Any habit or behavior that you need to do to be able to function normally could be described as an addiction. Whether that is alcohol, cigarettes, coffee, chocolate, drugs or checking your e-mails. So what exactly does it mean to have an addiction to something? Put simply, an addiction is when a person feels either physically or mentally dependent on a substance or a behavior, and they can't find a way to stop from continuing on with the addiction. If you have compulsions to engage in a particular kind of behavior and have withdrawal symptoms if you don't respond to the compulsion, you may be suffering from an addiction. Have you ever suffered from panic attacks, anxiety or palpitations when you are without your tech? What technology item can't you live without? Addictions not only place unnecessary stress on our bodies, they also cause stress when we do not have access to the substance or object to which we are addicted.

"Nomophobia"

Has the thought of having no signal on your cell phone ever caused you to break out in a cold sweat? Have you ever felt panicky or anxious when your mobile battery gets low? Have you ever experienced anxiety when out of cell phone contact with your friends, family or colleagues? If so, you are not alone—you are showing signs of a growing worldwide stress syndrome. The fear of losing mobile contact has become so common that experts have created a new term to describe the state of anxiety it creates for millions of people around the world—"nomophobia." This phobia is not just a fear of being out of mobile contact, it is also an addiction to your cell phone. If you know the panicked and disconnected feeling of leaving your mobile phone at home, you might be one of the many suffering from nomophobia.

E-mail

The advent of e-mail revolutionized our lives: we no longer had to wait days for important documents to arrive by mail or to send faxes. We could correspond across the planet instantaneously. However, this led to a massively increased flow of information and for many this can also be a cause of tech-stress. Many people are suffering from the growing problem of "e-mail stress" as they struggle to cope with an unending tide of messages—we feel tired, frustrated and unproductive after constantly monitoring the electronic messages that keep interrupting us as we attempt to concentrate on our work. People on a computer typically switch applications to view their e-mails as many as 30 or 40 times an hour, for anything from a few seconds to a minute. This really does drive home the astonishing extent to which e-mail has become embedded in our day-to-day lives in a relatively short period of time.

I get over 300 e-mails a day and sometimes I need to take a deep breath before opening my inbox. I have now had to discipline myself to open my inbox just a few times a day to check messages to reduce my stress levels, safeguard my health and stop feeling "invaded" by e-mails.

Many people that I work with feel stressed or overwhelmed by the sheer number of e-mails they receive and the obligation they feel to respond quickly. Do you see them as a source of pressure? If you sent an e-mail and you didn't get a response for a few days or a week, would you consider the recipient to be rude or lazy for tardiness in responding? Often we find ourselves under pressure to respond to e-mails more quickly to meet the expectations of the senders. This is where tech-stress can cause time stress.

E-mail is the thing that now causes us the most problems in our working lives. It's an amazing tool, but it's gotten out of hand. E-mail harries you. You want to know what's in that message, especially if it's from a family member or friend, or your boss, so you break from what you are doing to read the e-mail. The problem is that when you go back to what you were doing, you've lost your train of thought and, of course, you are less productive. People's brains get tired from taking a break from something every few minutes to check e-mails. The more distracted you are by distractions, the more tired you will be and the less productive. Bob Proctor, a productivity guru, suggests that distraction can hamper your productivity by over 500 percent. He states that you should work on one thing at a time and see it through to conclusion rather than jumping from task to task without completing any of them.

THE NUMBERS THAT DRIVE US CRAZY

- About **100 trillion** e-mail messages are sent worldwide every year.
- The average office worker spends **99 minutes** managing e-mails each day.
- Senior executives spend **4 hours** each day managing e-mails.
- **80 percent** of e-mails sent are actually "spam"—unsolicited advertisements, many of which are fraudulent or otherwise illegal.
- **62 percent** of workers check business e-mails while at home or on vacation.
- **20 percent** of workers are stressed.

Seven habits to control e-mail stress

1) **Don't be enslaved by your e-mail.**
   Never forget that e-mail is there to serve you. You can choose when to open your inbox or not, whether or not to respond to an e-mail and when you want to do so. You can save, file, archive or delete e-mails however you like.

2) **Put your e-mail into perspective.**

When was the last time you received a truly life-changing e-mail? A message that delivered a once-in-a-lifetime opportunity? An e-mail to say you have won the lottery jackpot or maybe a message from the Queen of England, who has decided to award you a knighthood? Do you regularly get those kinds of e-mails? The reality is that even if you did get those kinds of e-mails and you were "disconnected" for a few days, it wouldn't change much in the bigger scheme of things. Depending on your age, you may remember a time before we had e-mails on our phones being pinged to us 24/7—and if I recall correctly, we coped just fine—do remember that when things get too much!

3) **Choose your time to reduce e-mail stress.**

A lot of people have their e-mail inboxes open all the time—not just when they are sitting at their desks, on their phones also. They hear a "ping," a letter icon appears, or "you have mail" is shouted every time they receive a message. Or maybe the message pops up on your phone screen. This will inevitably cause constant distractions and breaks to your concentration and will also distract from more important work, take you in all sorts of directions and cause a lot of totally unnecessary tech-stress. You could be working on a quadrant 1 task and a quadrant 3 or 4 e-mail (see pages 138–39) comes in, preventing you from staying focused on the important urgent task at hand. Decide what time and for how long you are going to look at your e-mail. Once you have looked at your e-mail and dealt with any issues that have arisen from it, close your inbox. Many people look at their e-mail first thing before starting work or after being away from their desk for a while. Don't. It's more efficient and less distracting to do something first that requires your concentration—a quadrant 1 activity is preferable. Otherwise you might feel that your attention is pulled in many different directions right when you're at your most rested and effective.

4) **File/save important stuff right away.**

Many people flit from one message to another in their inboxes, saying to themselves that they will deal with them later. Does that sound like you? If so, make a point to deal with each e-mail as it comes. Save, file, delete or respond then and there and move on to the next one only when you have dealt with the first. Once each e-mail is dealt with, immediately file or delete the e-mail from your inbox.

5) **Process and purge.**

Once you have dealt with all your messages after an e-mail session, your inbox should be empty. This might sound impossible to you, but a completely empty inbox is something that you should aim for. It's no different to your desk or intray—lots of stuff lying around causes stress and is overwhelming, and the same goes for a full inbox. With an empty inbox, anything unimportant would have been deleted, everything else would have been filed away. I have four subfolders set up in my inbox, which are the same as the four quadrants of the prioritization grid in the previous chapter (see pages 138–39). As soon as I open my inbox, I sort them all into one of the four folders. I deal with the e-mails in box 1 (important and urgent) first, then when all the 1s are done, I move on to box 2. This way I am always working on the high-priority e-mails.

6) **Is your inbox your virtual attic?**

Many people have a space in their home—an attic, storage room or garage space—where things they don't need are kept. Do you? If so, reevaluate those things. If you haven't used them for a year, how important are they? It's likely that if you took these items down to your local charity shop, you wouldn't even miss them. Now think about your inbox. It is overloaded? Do you have e-mails in there dating back to 2009? Has your inbox become a place where you store unnecessary items—is it the attic of your computer? You need to regain control. In this case, during your e-mail session spend the first few minutes tidying up your old messages before you deal with the new ones. Don't rush this process—give yourself a few weeks to get everything straight. It may take time, but it will significantly reduce your level of stress.

7) **Stop panicking!**

If someone desperately wants or needs to get hold of you, they are not going to stop trying after sending just one e-mail. If it is really that urgent people will usually get on the phone—and you should adopt the same approach! Just because e-mail is instantaneous, it doesn't mean you have to respond to it instantaneously. Have a strategy to deal with e-mail—if there is other work to do that takes precedence over e-mail, consider switching e-mail off altogether. Always remember the golden rule—keep deleting to keep the number of new e-mails in your inbox to a minimum.

Your bridge can be seriously tested by the ongoing presence of excessive messages in your inbox—much of which can go unnoticed as it is running in the background. Take control, be ruthlessly brutal and put e-mail into perspective—much of your e-mails are 3rd and 4th quadrant messages and do not deserve to rob you of your valuable time!

DEAL WITH TECH-STRESS

With the growing pressures of modern technology, few of us are ever really "turned off" or inaccessible, and this is another major reason for tech-stress: if we don't turn off we don't have the much-needed time for rest and recovery. Always remember that technology is there to serve you, so if you are feeling overwhelmed, try these methods of dealing with tech-stress.

Disconnect from work

While people have always brought work home with them, in the days before e-mail, smartphones and the Internet, disconnecting from work was easier. Now we are more accessible, many of us spend valuable home time answering e-mails or work calls, and this is a major source of tech-stress.

This lack of downtime will not only prevent you from relaxing, it can also contribute to your stress levels. The way to combat this is to give yourself some time to disconnect from work.

- Tell your colleagues and work contacts that you will not be available after a certain time of day and you will deal with anything urgent when you are back at work. If you absolutely have to check your work e-mail, then do so as quickly as you can and respond only to the most urgent messages. Make sure that there are some times at home (during mealtimes or a couple of hours before bed) when your work phone is turned off.
- Make the most of your commute—with the right outlook you can use the time you spend traveling as a transition between your work life and home. If you drive, play soothing music, or read something light-hearted if you take public transport. And if you live close to work, running, walking or cycling home can also be a great stress reliever.
- Unwind by exercising, taking a leisurely walk, reading a great book or relaxing in the bathtub.

I aim to have my phone off from 10:00 p.m. to 8:00 a.m. each day. We also have a rule in our house—no mobiles or laptops in the bedroom (see also page 67 for more on why this is vital for sleep and as a means of stress prevention). We are working toward having no cell phones in the upstairs of our home.

Have the important conversations in person

As you are probably well aware, tone is notoriously difficult to detect in e-mail, IM or text messaging. This can lead to huge misunderstandings, hurt feelings or confusion. And often, sending a message via e-mail means that you are left waiting if your recipient is away from their desk, which can prolong stress and anxiety. If you need to have an important conversation (particularly those that fall in quadrants 1 and 2) (see pages 138–39) try to speak face to face, or at least over the phone. You will then be able to gauge tone much more easily and the potential for unnecessary drama and stress will be significantly reduced.

There is also another benefit to speaking in person. While technological advances in communication mean that we have more ways to speak to people, mediating our relationships through technology isn't desirable. Give your relationships a positive boost by taking the time for face-to-face conversation.

Choose your contacts wisely

Being overwhelmed and inundated with e-mail messages or reading constant and incessant social media updates from people who cause you stress in any way can easily ruin your mood. It is wise to be selective about who you are available to and when. I often feel obliged to accept any social media friend requests and used to hand over our personal contact details when asked; however, that resulted in several thousand Facebook friends and being added to groups I didn't choose to be a part of, and then receiving hundreds of e-mail updates from those groups. I have learned that it is okay to say no or ignore a request.

Alternatively, segment your contacts and only make yourself fully available to those you want to hear from regularly. For those people whom you'd rather you weren't constantly accessible to, try explaining to them politely that you rarely use that form of communication. It's also a good idea to set up separate accounts that you use to communicate with people such as colleagues.

I now have a professional page on most of my social media channels so people can connect and follow me; however, I am in control as to how I communicate with them to save being overwhelmed with messages, updates and being added to new groups.

Don't feel under pressure to have it all

Technology is constantly changing and evolving. For some of us this can be another major cause of tech-stress as we feel compelled to keep up with changes in technology. This could be described as technological "keeping up with the Joneses." It is important to realize that it is not essential to have and know it all. Although it is tempting to purchase the latest smartphone, tablet or computer, or to set up an account for every social media site in existence, remember that technology is meant to be there to enhance your life, not detract from it, and if it is causing you tech-stress, then it is not serving you. It is not worth letting technology negatively impact your life, so stick to what serves you and don't feel pressured to keep up with the latest trends.

Go on a digital detox

Many people spend most of their day in front of a computer, connected to the Internet or in some way engaged with our smartphone; however, this can lead to us feeling disconnected from our surroundings and the people in our lives. This "disengagement" as a result of tech-stress can also lead to us missing out on the joyful experiences of daily life, such as real conversations with the people around us and taking in the pleasures of our surroundings.

To minimize tech-stress and make time for more worthwhile activities, have a digital detox. Spend a week, day or afternoon (whatever is feasible—or you can handle) without any technology and live in the real world instead. Take in the sounds of the environment around you, rather than being plugged in to your iPod; look at the view, rather than your phone screen; meet up with people, rather than texting them. You will find that the world doesn't fall apart just because you are away from technology for a while. And check your stress levels afterward—they're probably greatly decreased.

When on vacation avoid or limit checking messages and e-mail so you can have a true break. If you must check messages, leave your phone in your hotel and have a specific time when you can check messages—and limit that time to 15–30 minutes. There are hotels now that frown on using phones by the pool or in common areas—that is, tapping away on them as well as speaking on them.

MY PERSONAL ACTION PLAN

I promise myself I am going to master the technology in my life by taking these actions:

1. _____

2. _____

3. _____

4. _____

5. _____

Enter your commitments in your well-being journal to log your actions and progress.

CHAPTER 14

STEP 10:

Learn to say no

You already have a huge pile of work to deal with, you have to rush off at 5:30 p.m. to pick up your children from the babysitter, then you have to go home and make dinner. Just as you are getting ready to dash out the door your boss shouts over at you (while on the phone to a client) and informs you that he needs that report, which was due tomorrow afternoon, before you leave tonight. You reluctantly agree, knowing that you can't just leave without doing it and if you are going to have to wait for him to get off the phone (he looks like he's going to be a while) you may as well just finish the report. You are now stressed: you are late, you have hungry children and an angry babysitter. I call this "yes-stress." Stress caused by agreeing to do something that at that particular time you don't have the capacity for. Someone else's task has been delegated to you, which causes your stress levels to spike.

ASSESS YOUR ASSERTIVENESS

I take on far more than I can deal with.	Y/N
I feel people take advantage of me.	Y/N
I agree to things to avoid confrontation.	Y/N
I regularly feel stressed because of tasks that others have given me.	Y/N

If you answered yes to all or most of those questions, you need some help. This chapter will give you a great start, with many practical suggestions on improving your assertiveness and saying no when it's appropriate to prevent your bridge becoming overburdened.

WHY WE FIND IT HARD TO SAY NO

To learn to say no, we have to first understand why we resist it. Below are some common reasons that people find it hard to say no:

- **You don't want to let people down and you genuinely want to help**. You are a kind soul at heart. You struggle to turn the person away and you are willing to help where possible, even if it distracts you, eats into your time and causes you "yes-stress."
- **Concerned about being rude**. I was brought up with the belief that saying no, especially to people who are older or more senior, is extremely rude. This thinking is common in many cultures, where saving face is important. Saving face means not making others look bad.
- **Desire to conform.** You don't want to alienate yourself from the group because you're not in agreement. So you agree to the requests of others.
- **Fear of conflict**. I often used to agree to things just to avoid confrontation or conflict. I was concerned the person may be angry if I rejected them. I also was concerned that even if there wasn't a confrontation there could be an element of dissent, which could have future consequences.
- **Fear of opportunities lost**. Another reason for worrying could be that saying no may result in turning your back on opportunities. For example, my friend was asked to transfer to another department in her company. She liked her team so she didn't want to move. However, she didn't want to say no, as she felt it would affect her promotion opportunities in the future.

- **Not burning bridges**. Some people perceive a no as a sign of rejection. There is a fear it might lead to bridges being burned and relationships being severed.

In my experience these reasons are misconceptions. They are all false beliefs. At the end of the day, it's more about *how* you say no, rather than the fact that you're saying it, which affects the outcome. After all, you have your own priorities and needs, just like everyone has or his her own needs. Saying no is about respecting and valuing your time and space. Saying no is your prerogative.

EVALUATE REQUESTS

It's not always easy to determine which activities deserve your time and attention. Use these strategies to evaluate obligations—and opportunities—that are presented to you.

- **Focus on the things that are most important to you.** Take a good look at your existing commitments and overall priorities before making any new ones. Consider how important the new commitment is to you. If it's something you feel strongly about, go ahead and do it. If not, reject it diplomatically.
- **Weigh the yes-stress ratio.** Is the new activity you're pondering a short- or long-term commitment? For example, turning up to support your child's soccer matches will take far less time than agreeing to coach them all season. Don't make commitments if it will add months and months of stress. Instead, consider other ways that you can contribute.
- **Remove guilt from the equation.** Don't agree to something if your gut instinct is to say no, especially if you are only agreeing due to feelings of guilt or out of obligation. Otherwise you are setting yourself up for additional stress and resentment.

- **Sleep on it.** Are you tempted by an invitation to join a weekly tennis club, or volunteer for a charity? Don't make the commitment immediately—before agreeing, take a day or two to think about it and assess how it fits into your schedule with your preexisting commitments.

WHY SAY NO?

In Chapter 12 we introduced the prioritization grid (see pages 138–39). Often people will approach you with tasks that are in their first quadrant. That doesn't necessarily mean they are in *your* first quadrant. Just because something is important and urgent to them it doesn't mean it also is for you. Is your bridge already heavily burdened with deadlines and obligations that you're trying to squeeze into the few hours you have before you go home? Are you trying to cram too many activities into too little time? If so, taking yourself from distress to de-stress can be as straightforward as just saying no. Consider the following reasons for saying no:

- **Saying no doesn't mean you are being selfish.** When you say no to a new task, you're honoring your existing commitments and this also ensures that you are able to devote quality time to them.
- **Saying no can allow you to pursue new things.** Just because you've always helped plan the company Christmas party doesn't mean that you have to keep doing it forever. Saying no will give you time to pursue other interests or activities.
- **Yes is not always the healthiest answer.** When you're overcommitted and under too much stress, you're more likely to feel run down and even get ill—remember what happens to a bridge with too much load on it!
- **Saying yes can prevent others from stepping up.** It prevents people from taking responsibility and can lead to them feeling

cut off. It will prevent them from stepping up. On the other hand, when you say no you open the door for others to progress and benefit from doing that task or activity. They may not do things exactly the way you would, but that's okay. They'll find their own way. It will also support their learning and development.

LEARN HOW TO SAY NO

I personally have a tough time saying no to people; it's always harder to say no than yes, but where a no is the appropriate response, it's important to learn to say it without guilt. Let's look at how you can better equip yourself to use no as an appropriate response to prevent "yes-stress." Here are some things to keep in mind when you need to say no:

- **Saying no with confidence.** "No" is a very powerful word. Use it confidently and without fear. Be careful about using weak phrases to replace no, such as "I'm not sure," "I don't think so," "maybe," "possibly." These can be interpreted as "I might say yes later."
- **Saying no with brevity.** Be clear regarding your reason for refusing the request, but don't get involved in extended discussions about it. Avoid elaborate justifications or explanations.
- **Saying no honestly.** Don't make up excuses to get out of a commitment. Being truthful is the best way to turn someone down.
- **Saying no respectfully.** You may have many important or good causes that are put in front of you and sometimes it is tough to turn them down. Acknowledging and complimenting the efforts of the group while informing them that you are unable to commit at this time will show them you respect their endeavors.
- **Saying no repeatedly.** When refusing a request, occasionally you may find that you have to repeat your response several times before it is accepted by the other. If you do experience this, just

calmly and firmly repeat your response and if necessary you can reaffirm your original reasons behind why you declined.

If you are used to saying yes, then getting into the habit of saying no whenever it's appropriate to do so will be difficult to begin with. But don't worry—it will get easier, especially once you have seen how beneficial the little word "no" can be to your life! So many of us overload our bridges, which, as we have seen, is a major stressor, and yet by saying yes we take on more and more until our bridge is buckling with the strain. Just learning to use that little word "no" will help your levels of stress—and improve your self-confidence and self-esteem immeasurably.

Easy ways to say no

Avoid suffering from "yes-stress" by learning effective ways in which to say no. Once I got used to saying no to others, I realized that it wasn't as difficult as I had made it out to be in my mind! In fact, when I said no most people were very understanding and didn't force the issue. As I know that the prospect of saying no can be stressful, here are some lines to use, to get you started.

1) **"I'm too busy to take on any more commitments at the moment."**
This is what I say when I have too much to do and people are making requests on my time. If you feel it would help them to understand your situation, you can share with them what you are currently focusing on and what load is on your bridge.

2) **"I'm right in the middle of something at the moment, so how about we connect at X time?"**
I often get sudden or urgent requests when I am doing something. I could be writing a report and a colleague will approach me with a

question, or I may get a phone call from a friend or family member when I'm in a meeting. This reply holds off the request until you are ready to deal with it. It lets the person know it's not a good time as you are busy, and you haven't put him or her off as you've suggested a time when you're going to respond to the question.

3) **"I'd love to do this, but . . ."**

I often get offers to partner with people which, for a variety of reasons, I can't take on. This is a softer way of saying no. I might feel that their ideas are absolutely fantastic, but due to other commitments, I can't take them on. This reply means that it keeps the lines of communication open, so that I haven't burned my bridges if I want to work with them in the future. It's worth saying that you should use this reply only if you really do like the ideas. You should always be honest when you are saying no to something.

4) **"Let me think about it and I'll get back to you."**

This means you don't have to make a decision on the spot. Technically this isn't a no, its more of a maybe. If you are genuinely interested, but aren't sure if you can take the commitment on or don't have enough information to make an informed decision, this is a great response to use. Often I'm approached with a great idea that fits with our current aspirations; however, I will use this response if I need time to think about it or I am already busy with something else and cannot give anything new my full focus and attention. When you take the time to consider the opportunity carefully, new challenges may present themselves, and I want to have explored all the pros and cons before committing myself or my team. If the person making the request is sincere and genuine they should be happy to wait a short while. Be clear about the date/time by which they can expect a reply. If you are not interested in what they have to offer, don't lead them on, instead use the responses below, which are clear and definitive.

5) **"This doesn't meet my current needs; however, I'll be sure to keep you in mind."**

If someone is suggesting a collaboration or opportunity that isn't what you are currently seeking, let them know straightaway that it doesn't meet your needs. Failing to do so can lead to discussions that drag on far longer than they should or need to. Let them know there's nothing wrong with what they are offering, it's just that you are looking for something else. As you have stated, you will keep them in mind, making it clear that you are still open to future opportunities.

6) **"I don't think that I am the best person to help on this. Why don't you try X?"**

You may find that you are approached to do something but you don't have the expertise or resources to take it on. It's best in this case to let them know that they are considering the wrong person. If you know someone who is a better fit for what they want, then refer them to that person. I always feel it's best to try and suggest someone else who might help, so that the person doesn't end up stuck without any way of addressing their task. This way at least you can help point them in the right direction.

7) **"No, I'm sorry, I can't."**

Sometimes it's better not to think about saying no and just to come out and say it in a firm and direct manner. We can often construct too many obstacles in our own minds to saying no, and sometimes they're not as insurmountable as we believe. In fact, once you have said no in such a direct way, you may find that you are pleasantly surprised by the person's response.

Once you have learned to say no, you'll quickly discover just how easy it is, but also you'll find that you'll have more time for yourself, your work and the things you find most important. It's worked out well for me, and I'm happy I learned to deal with my yes-stress.

Dealing with the push people

You may find that you will get someone who responds to your no with: "What do you mean no? Why can't you do it? It will take only 15 minutes." This is where I often struggle, and in the past I would concede. It is *only* 15 minutes. But four 15-minute requests is an hour, and 16 equates to 4 hours. They can add up very quickly, and before you know it a big chunk of your time has been used up. The best advice I can offer is to have an affirmation you can use in such situations, for example: "Thank you and I am flattered that you feel so passionately about me being involved, it's just I have so much other stuff on my plate at the moment that I just can't give you my commitment and guarantee I will be able to deliver the results that you need. There is a good chance I will fail to deliver my best results and within the time frames you need to achieve. I would rather say 'no' at this time, rather than 'I'm sorry' at a later stage."

MY PERSONAL ACTION PLAN

I promise myself I am going to decrease my yes-stress by taking these actions:

1. _____

2. _____

3. _____

4. _____

5. _____

Enter your commitments in your well-being journal to log your actions and progress.

CHAPTER 15

PUTTING THE 10-STEP STRESS SOLUTION INTO ACTION

Have you ever heard the saying "knowledge is power"? Do you believe it? I used to believe it too. I knew that I needed to amass knowledge so I could fulfill my mission to change the lives of millions of people. I took courses, bought hundreds of books, invested in CD and DVD training programs. I recently calculated that in a couple of years I had invested over $70,000 in personal development activities. Yet, even though I had amassed a wealth of knowledge, I hadn't become rich and successful, my relationships weren't as amazing as I would have liked them to be and I wasn't running a massive business empire.

It was then that it dawned on me. Simply amassing knowledge doesn't make you powerful; it just turns you into a walking encyclopedia. If you want to turn knowledge into power there is one more important and valuable step that must be taken: you need to take action! However little those steps may be, they will take you on a different path to the one that you are currently on. Even adjusting your trajectory by a few inches today will result in you ending up in a totally different destination.

APPLY THE KNOWLEDGE TO BECOME POWERFUL

How are you going to apply what you have learned in this book? How will you turn this knowledge into power?

At the end of each of the 10 steps you completed a personal action plan. Let us now bring these together and create a set of goals from which you can draw up your final action plan. Setting goals will ensure you utilize the knowledge you have gained—it sets out a means of putting theory into practice and turning knowledge into action. I have a goal-setting process to ensure you come up with some excellent goals.

Define your goals

Firstly, you need to recognize and define your goals. The process below is a method for defining a goal and then checking to see if the goal will work.

1) Where do you want to be, or what do you want to achieve?
2) How will you know when you have succeeded?
3) What will the effects be on you and those around you?
4) What resources do you need to succeed?
5) Do you have the resources or access to these resources?
6) What has prevented you from doing anything about this before?
7) How can you stop it happening this time?
8) Final check—is this all you can achieve, want or desire?

Clarify your goals

A specific, well-defined goal has a much greater chance of being accomplished than a general goal. A useful tool for clarifying our goals is the "SMARTO" framework, as outlined below.

S **SPECIFIC**: A goal to "be happier" is nonspecific, indefinable and impossible to quantify. Whereas "to get up at 6:30 a.m. instead of 7:30 a.m. every morning, so that I can be in the office an hour earlier" is specific.

M **MEASURABLE**: It's impossible to tell if the goal has been achieved if it can't be measured. It's also encouraging, especially as the goal may take some time to achieve fully, if the progress toward the goal can be measured. For example, "I will lose 11 pounds by July 10."

A **ACHIEVABLE**: The goal has to be realistic. Attempting a goal that isn't achievable will result only in disappointment. It's pointless for someone with a numeracy problem to enroll in a degree program in mathematics, for example. By adjusting the goal to enrolling in math classes, you're attempting something with a realistic chance of success, which may or may not lead to a desire for further achievement.

R **REALISTIC/RELEVANT**: The goal must be relevant to you and your situation. Going for long walks in the countryside may be enjoyable, but it's hardly relevant for someone who is trying to meet new people.

T **TIME**: There must be a specific period over which either the entire goal, or a specific part of the goal, will be achieved. If goals are likely to take too long, they should be broken down into stages, so that you can see quite clearly how far you have progressed.

O **OWN**: The goal MUST be your own, rather than a goal someone else has set for you, otherwise it's unlikely to succeed or sustain.

"I will run the marathon next April in less than four hours" is a SMARTO goal for me. Someone asking (or telling) me to run the marathon next year is not my goal, so I may not take full ownership of it and in turn may struggle to achieve it.

In your well-being journal take some time to come up with 10 goals that you would like to achieve based on what you have learned in this book. Take some time with this and dare to think big. Examples include:

- I will only take on new tasks if they are in the first quadrant in my prioritization grid (see pages 138–39).
- I will spend 45 minutes unwinding at the end of every day to avoid struggling to fall asleep at night.
- I will go to sleep by 10:00 or 10:30 p.m. every day to maximize the benefits of my time asleep.
- I will fill in my prioritization grid every day for one month and leave work on time to focus on becoming more relaxed at work.
- I will incorporate relaxation, such as meditation or yoga, into my everyday routine.

There could also be things that you need to do or actions you need to take—"sub goals," if you like—that may need to be achieved in order to fulfill a bigger goal. Examples include:

- I will research yoga classes online by the end of the month.
- I will register for a workshop within the next six weeks.

MY PERSONAL ACTION PLAN

I promise myself I am going to apply the 10-step stress solution, and turn knowledge into power by achieving these goals.

1. _____

2. _____

3. _____

4. _____

5. _____

6. _____

7. _____

8. _____

9. _____

10. _____

Enter your commitments in your well-being journal to log your actions and progress.

Remember the bridge metaphor from Chapter 1? Nobody is born with a naturally strong bridge, but we do all have the ability to develop a stronger, more resilient bridge. Be aware of the load on your bridge and ask yourself some questions. Are you coping with the demand? Are you bowing and buckling due to overload? If so, what steps can you take to alleviate the load? Or what can you do to better support the bridge? How can you utilize the 10-step stress solution to better equip you to cope with the stress and challenges of life?

Remember, power can literally be defined as the ability to do something. A victim is powerless as there is nothing they can do to change their situation. Take back your power and control of your stress by applying the 10-step stress solution. My belief is that we are the most powerful beings in our universe. Setting the belief that you are an all-powerful being in turn empowers you to make decisions and brings about change in your life. Tap into your inner power, make some commitments to yourself and review them regularly. Continue taking action and it is only a matter of time before you are leading the happy, healthy, stress-free life you deserve!

FURTHER SUPPORT

www.feelkarma.com
Products that can aid in recognizing and reducing stress.

www.mind.org.uk
A UK-based mental health charity.

www.breathing-exercises.com
Provides information about breathing exercises and breathing development techniques, which are extremely helpful in overcoming various kinds of challenges.

www.sleepcouncil.org.uk
Offers lots of advice on how to improve your sleep.

www.stress.org.uk
The Stress Management Society. Useful support, advice and guidance to better understand how you can recognize and deal with stress in your life.

www.stressmanagementsociety.com
Support for companies wishing to tackle workplace stress.

www.timemanagement.com
Free time-management tips and software to help you manage your time.

ACKNOWLEDGMENTS

I would like to start by saying a massive and heartfelt thank you to Louise Francis from Vermilion for all of her support and flexibility in getting this book completed. I am sure I caused you stress with my multiple requests for extensions to the deadline.

I appreciate all the efforts and patience Imogen Fortes and Justine Taylor showed in getting my manuscript ready for publishing.

I would like to thank my amazing team for forgiving my extended absences from the office while I was busy writing, in particular Ranjit Patel, Simran Braich, Anisha Rawal, Sheli Rawal, Dee Varsani and Lettica Phillips for covering my workload when I had locked myself in my study to write.

I would like to thank my colleague Andrea Sangster for all her support over the years and also her guidance in shaping the ideas for this book in its earlier incarnations.

A heartfelt thanks to my business partner Kit Shah: his unending support and belief in me and my abilities is one of the primary reasons that I can enjoy the level of success that I have achieved. I am sure I have been a cause of much stress in your life and I cannot begin to tell you how much I value your support.

To Hash and Steve, a heartfelt thanks for being there when I needed support to my bridge and helping me to keep me strong.

I would like to thank everyone who has ever supported me and my work—my friends, my family, my clients, the people that attend my workshops and everyone else who has contributed to this rich journey that is my life.

And, finally, thank you so much, Nivi, for showing up when you did.

Love life and smile.

INDEX

acne 93
act as if 120
addiction 148
adenosine 40
adrenaline 16–17, 25, 30, 40, 42, 57, 64, 69
alarm clocks 69
alcohol/drinking 12, 15, 31, 35, 36–37, 42, 48, 62, 148
    stimulant and depressant effects 36–37
almonds 99, 100
alveoli 74
anger 14, 23, 24, 49, 110, 123
anger management 84
antidepressants 4
antioxidants 102–3
anxiety 14, 15, 23, 37, 38, 41, 49
    benefits of camomile 103
    benefits of exercise 108, 109–10
    benefits of mindful breathing 82
    incompatible with relaxation 27
    and shallow breathing 72, 75, 76
    and tech stress 148, 155
    and time stress 134, 137
apples 104–5
aromatherapy baths 65
arteries 48, 49, 72, 74
artificial sweeteners 92
asparagus 102
avocados 103

bananas 102
Beech, Simone 83
beef 102
beta-carotene 103

beta-endorphins 108
blackout curtains 69
bladder relaxation 14, 24
Blair, Tony 3
Blake, William 5
blood pressure see high blood pressure; hypertension
blood sugar
    and diet 96, 97, 101, 105
    and relaxation 27
    and stress 9, 14, 22, 24, 41
body clock 69
brain
    benefits of omega-3 fatty acids 100
    benefits of theanine 101
    chemical messengers 42, 101
    effects of water 88
    oxygen consumption 72
    sleep associations 65–66
    SOS signals 14
    temporary shutdown of higher functions 18–19
brain-balancing breathing technique 79–81
breathing 71–86
    assessment 71
    deep and slow 27, 75
    how it works 74
    long-distance runners 116
    overcoming panic attacks (case study) 83
    shallow and fast 14, 17, 24, 26, 75–76
    and smoking 38
    test your breath 75
    see also oxygen

breathing exercises 65, 76–85, 120
  1: natural breath 77–78
  2: breathing for stress relief 78–79
  3: alternated nostril breathing
    79–81
  4: mindful breathing 81–84
  5: energizing breathing 84–85
bridge metaphor 10–12
broccoli 100
bronchi 74
bronchioles 74
Buddhist monks 5

caffeine 35, 39–40, 42, 62, 91, 96, 101
calcium 99
camomile 103
cancer 37, 47, 50
Cannon, Walter 8–9
carbohydrates 17, 40, 97, 103
carbon dioxide 74, 75
cardiac arrest 51
Caveman Joe 9, 14, 30, 35–36
children 64–65, 77
chocolate 35, 36, 40, 42, 58, 62, 98, 148
  dark 100
cholesterol 48
cigarettes/smoking 12, 15, 35,
    37–39, 42, 48, 148
circulation 27, 47, 49, 64, 69
cocoa, drinking 101
coffee 31, 36, 39, 42, 64, 84, 98, 148
colds and flu 15, 19, 52
commute time 154
concentration problems 39, 96, 123,
    135
constipation 21, 99
consumerism 28
cortisol 25, 41, 69, 110
  and caffeine 40
  and dehydration 88, 90
  effects on the body 17, 22
  maintaining low levels 57, 64, 100

counseling 4, 33

death zone 73
defocusing 129
depression 4, 15, 36, 37, 47, 72, 108,
    123, 135
diabetes, type-2 47, 96, 100
diaphragm 74, 77
diarrhea 21, 37
digestion
  and relaxation 27
  and stress 49
  temporary shutdown 21
digestive problems 21, 47, 49
digital detox 156–57
dopamine 40, 42
dreaming 59
drug taking 12, 15, 48, 148
dust mites 66–67

eating disorders 48
electronic devices, evicting from the
    bedroom 67, 154–55
e-mail 149–53
  controlling e-mail stress
    150–53
  statistics 150
emotions
  effect on the heart 49
  heeding 123–24
  releasing through exercise
    109–10
  response to stress 23
endorphins 65, 100, 101, 108, 109
erectile dysfunction 22
Everest, Mount 5, 73
evolution 9
exercise 107–17
  assessment 107–8
  avoiding close to bedtime 64
  and fitness 50
  forms 111–12

and mental state 109, 120
sprint vs. marathon 112–17
and stress relief 108–12
exercise buddies 110–11
exhaustion 4, 15, 16

face-to-face conversations 155
fat(s) 94, 96, 97, 99, 102
and energy supply 17, 22, 105
monounsaturated 103
as primary fuel source 40–41
fatigue and tiredness 12, 16, 39, 88,
90, 96, 103, 135
fears and phobias 82–4 see also
"nomophobia"
fertility 23
fiber, dietary 99, 103
fight-or-flight 8–9, 13, 17, 21, 22, 25,
107, 109, 134
fish
oily 99, 104
white 102
fitness vs. health 49–51
case study 52
folic acid 100, 102
food and diet 94–106
assessment 95
breakfast 96–97
constant picking at food 98–99
eating little and often 105
eating mindfully 81–82
and energy levels (case study) 98
and the nervous system 104
rainbow foods 104
skipping meals 97–98, 105
and stress 95–105
stress-busting foods 99–103
toxins 94, 104–5
formaldehyde 92
"freeze" state 134
fruit and vegetables 58, 97,
99, 104

ghrelin 57
glucagon 105
glucose 17, 22 see also blood sugar
goals 169–72
clarification (SMARTO) 169–70
defining 169
grandmother's feat of strength 30
green tea 91, 98, 101
guided imagery 130

hangovers 37
headaches 12, 20, 37, 88, 90, 91, 103,
109, 135
health 46–54
assessment 46
benefits of sleep 57–59
improving 51–53
poor health and stress 47–48
health vs. fitness 49–51
case study 52
heart (cardiovascular system), and
stress 47–49
heart attacks 16, 48
heart disease
protective factors 50, 99, 100
risk factors 40, 47, 48, 95
heart rate
and relaxation 27
and stress 9, 14, 17, 48, 90
herbal tea 91
high blood pressure
benefits of relaxation 27
benefits of stroking pets 65
and caffeine 40
foods to control 102, 103
guided imagery treatment 130
and nicotine withdrawal 38
and stress 9, 14, 17, 24, 47, 48–49, 95
hobbies 125
hormones 47
and caffeine 39
sexual 64

hormones (*cont.*)
  weight control 57
  see also stress hormones
Hyde, Steven 63
hydration 87–93
  assessment 87
  daily water requirements 89
  importance of water 87, 88–89
  signs of dehydration 88–89
  and stress reduction 89–91, 101
  see also sodas
hydrochloric acid 17, 92
hypertension 47, 48

Idzikowski, Chris 62
immune system
  boosting 27, 50, 102–3, 104, 130
  effects of caffeine 40
  effects of stress 16, 47, 95
  and sleep 57
  temporary shutdown 19
impotence 38
indigestion 21
insomnia *see* sleep
insulin 22
intercostal muscles 74, 77
iron 102
irritability 12, 38, 39, 56, 72, 81, 103,
  135
irritable bowel syndrome (IBS) 47,
  49, 103

Kabat-Zinn, Jon 81
knowledge
  insufficient for power 168
  turning into power 169–73

lactobacillus 99
leptin 57
lettuce 103
libido (sex drive), temporary loss
  21–23

looking good 110
lung cancer 37
lungs 38, 74, 77, 79
magnesium 99, 100, 103, 104
marathon running 50
  and health (case study) 52
  and mindset (case study)
    125–28
  vs. sprinting 112–17
martial arts 111–12
massage 33, 64, 65
meditation 52, 69, 124, 171
  at bedtime 65
  moving 112
medulla oblongata (primitive/
    reptilian brain) 18, 72, 134
melatonin 69, 102
memory, benefits of sleep 59
  case study 68
memory lapses 135
mind, body and spirit 49–50, 53
mindful breathing 81–84
mindfulness 81
mindset 118–32
  assessment 118
  benefits of exercise 109, 120
  erasing negative thoughts 122–23
  harnessing the power of the mind
    121–22
  heeding your emotions 123–24
  and marathon running (case
    study) 125–28
  mental relaxation 124–25
  and physiology 119–20
  using self-hypnosis 129–32
mineral supplement 104
minerals 96, 99, 104
mobile phones 148
mood
  benefits of exercise 108–9, 110
  nutrients to stabilize 102
mood swings 36, 39, 96, 135

mountaineering 5, 73
moving house 122–23
Muamba, Fabrice 51
muscles
  benefits of sleep 58–59
  progressive muscle relaxation
    (PMR) 113–15
  relaxed 27
  tense 17, 24, 109

nausea 12, 21, 37, 90
nervous system 14, 49, 103, 104, 108
neurotransmitters 102
nicotine 37–39, 62
"nomophobia" 146
nuts 99–100, 104

omega-3 fatty acids 99, 100
oranges 101–2
organic food 105
overeating 12, 15, 22
oxygen 47, 71, 72, 74, 75, 76
  hazards of lack (case study) 73

pain, temporary shutdown 19–21
panic attacks 16, 82, 148
  overcoming with breathing (case
    study) 83
planning 136, 141, 143
pleasant memory technique 129–30
porridge 101
positive affirmations 131–32
positive thinking 121–25
post-traumatic stress disorder 20
posture 120
potassium 102, 103
power
  knowledge alone insufficient 168
  turning knowledge into 169–73
prana 76
pranayama 76
prioritization grid 138–40
  and goal-setting 171

and saying no 161
and sorting e-mails 152
prioritizing 136–40
Proctor, Bob 150
progressive muscle relaxation
  (PMR) 113–15
protein(s) 58, 97, 101, 105
prunes 102–3

red blood cells 74
refined sugar see sugar
relaxation
  goal-setting 171
  mental 124–25
  physical and psychological
    benefits 27
relaxing in the sunshine technique
  130
REM sleep 56–57, 59
resilience to stress 111
respiratory center 72
rooibos tea 91
running
  benefits for sleep (case study) 63
  outside 110
  see also marathon running

sabertooth tiger attacks 9, 14, 17–19,
  21, 23, 35–36, 41
salmon 100
saying no 137, 158–67
  assertiveness assessment 158
  dealing with the push people 166
  easy ways 163–64
  evaluating requests 160–61
  learning how 162–66
  reasons for 161–62
  why we find it hard 159–60
self-confidence 108, 110, 125, 163
self-esteem 110, 125, 163
self-hypnosis 128–32
Selye, Hans 9

serotonin 42, 101, 102
sexual intercourse 64 *see also* libido
Shah, Neil 52, 73, 92–93, 125–28
sighing after stress 25–26
skin
  and hydration 87, 91
  and stress 17
sleep 55–70
  assessment 55
  beneficial foods 102, 103
  benefits of exercise 108
  benefits of running (case study) 63
  creating a sleep haven 65–67
  effects of caffeine 40
  goal-setting 171
  guided imagery for insomnia 130
  how much is needed 59–60
  improving 60–70
  looking after your inner child
    64–65
  and mental capacity (case study) 68
  and mental relaxation 124
  as nature's healer 56–59
  preparing your body for 62–64
  stages 56–57
  using your senses 67–69
  and weight loss (case study) 58
  what night is best? 60
  when to go to bed 60
sleep diary 61
Slow Burn (Mittleman) 52
smells, sleep-inducing 67
smiling 119–20
social interaction, and exercise
  110–11
social media, choosing your
  contacts 155–56
sodas 40, 88
  replacing with water 91
  replacing with water (case study)
    92–93
Solanki, Ricky 98

soldier's experience (pain shutdown)
  20
spinach 103
sports 112
  and mental relaxation 125
sports people, professional 50–51
sprint vs. marathon 112–17
stage fright 82
starting the day 69–70
stimulants 35–41
  and sleep 62
  why the body craves when
    stressed 41–43
stomach
  "butterflies" 14
  effects of excess hydrochloric acid
    17
  knotting 24
stomach pains 21
stress
  defining 8–12
  emotional response 23
  as a help 29–30
  as a hindrance 30–31
  modern definition 10–12
  physical experience of 24–26
  and poor health 47–49
  positive aspects 9–10
  resilience to 111
  signs of 12
  stimulants as coping mechanisms
    35–43
  symptoms caused by poor time
    management 135
  vulnerability test 31–34
  what happens in the body 16–23
stress hormones 9, 22, 102
  burning off 26, 64, 108
  see also adrenaline; cortisol
Stress Management Society 3, 5, 10,
  24, 35
  Web sites 33, 175

stress stages 13–16
  stage 1: alarm 14–15
  stage 2: resistance 15
  stage 3: exhaustion 16
stressors 13
  long-term "chronic" 13
  short-term "acute" 13
stroke 47, 48
subconscious mind 128–29
sugar(s), refined 35, 42, 62, 94,
    96–97, 99, 100, 101
  as emergency fuel 40–41
survival state 28
sweat glands and sweating 9, 24, 27
sweet potatoes 103
swimming 112
system shutdown 17–23

tea 31, 39, 98
technology 146–57
  assessment 146
  dealing with tech-stress 153–57
  and disruption of plans 136
  and stress 148–53
temperature, bedroom 69
Thatcher, Margaret 59
theanine 101
time management 133–45
  assessment 133
  effective 135–40
  myths 141
time management exercises 143–45
  1: become a better estimator
    143–44
  2: power time log 144–45
time robbers 141–42
  TOP principle 142
time stress
  principles of good management
    143
  symptoms 143
  and tech stress 149

toxins in food 94, 104–5
trachea 74
triglycerides 48
tryptophan 101
turkey 101

ulcers 49

Viagra 23
vitamin supplements 104
vitamins 19, 96, 99, 103, 104, 105
  B 99, 102, 104
  B3 102
  C 101–2, 104
  E 99

walking 112
water *see* hydration
water filters 90
Watkins, Janette 58
weight
  and nut consumption 100
  and sleep 57–58
  and stress 22
weight loss
  and exercise 110
  and sleep (case study) 58
well-being journal 26, 91
  goal-setting 171
  personal action plans 54, 93, 70,
    106, 117, 132, 145, 157, 167, 172
  sleep diary 61
  "sub-goals" 171
Welsh, Aegon 68
white noise 68
work, disconnecting from 154–55

yes-stress 158, 159, 160, 162, 163, 166
yoga 33, 52, 69, 76, 79, 111, 120, 171
yogurt 99

zinc 102, 104

ABOUT THE AUTHOR

Neil Shah is the founder and director of The Stress Management Society and one of the UK's leading authorities on stress management and well-being issues. He is a stress-management consultant and motivational speaker, is a qualified practitioner of hypnotherapy and counseling, and has trained in neuro-linguistic programming (NLP). Neil has helped thousands of people tackle stress through one-on-one coaching and workshops, and travels all over the world to teach stress-management techniques.